James Mavor, Simon J. McLean

The Tariff History of Canada

James Mavor, Simon J. McLean

The Tariff History of Canada

ISBN/EAN: 9783337190149

Printed in Europe, USA, Canada, Australia, Japan

Cover: Foto ©Suzi / pixelio.de

More available books at **www.hansebooks.com**

TORONTO UNIVERSITY STUDIES.

IN

POLITICAL SCIENCE

JAMES MAVOR, Editor.

———————

No. IV.

THE TARIFF HISTORY OF CANADA

BY

SIMON J. McLEAN, B.A.,

Mackenzie Fellow in Political Science,

University of Toronto.

WITH A PREFACE

BY

JAMES MAVOR,

Professor of Political Economy and Constitutional History, University of Toronto. Formerly Professor of Political Economy and Statistics, St. Mungo's College, Glasgow.

TORONTO:
WARWICK BROS. & RUTTER, PRINTERS, &c., 68 & 70 FRONT STREET WEST.
1895.

TORONTO UNIVERSITY STUDIES IN POLITICAL SCIENCE·

W. J. ASHLEY, Editor.

JAMES MAVOR, Editor.

*Copies of these Essays may be obtained on application to the Education Department for Ontario,
Toronto.*

TABLE OF CONTENTS.

PREFACE

The Toronto University Studies in Political Science were instituted by Professor Ashley in 1889. Three monographs were published in that series, each of them being a valuable study in Canadian economic or constitutional history.

The present issue consists of a History of the Canadian Tariff, by Mr. Simon J. McLean, B.A., Mackenzie Fellow in Political Science. This monograph is expanded from a paper written in competition for the Bankers' Scholarship in 1894. Mr. McLean divided the prize with Mr. J. D. Phillips, B.A., the papers of these two competitors being regarded as equal.

Although the tariff and its history involve many political as well as economic considerations; and although the statement of these is not easy without disclosing a bias towards one or the other of the political parties, an attempt has been made in the following pages to give an impartial account of the history of the tariff.

Academic treatment of problems that are always in the melting pot of political controversy, must necessarily appear tame and bald beside the rhetoric of partisans; but its value for the student is none the less on that account. Clear statement of the dry bones is an indispensable preliminary to the formation of reliable conclusions; and it appears to me that Mr. McLean has successfully accomplished this.

Mr. McLean has brought together for the first time, the elements which contributed both before and after confederation towards the making of the tariff as it now is. He has shewn that one of the main reasons for confederation was the "commercial union" of the provinces. He has shewn, also, that although the provincial tariffs prior to 1867 were very varied, they were in the main low tariffs for revenue rather than high tariffs for protection. This feature of the provincial tariffs, especially those of the Maritime Provinces, practically determined the character of the Dominion tariff when confederation brought the provinces together. Mr. McLean has also shewn how after the early days of confederation were over, the country, under the guidance of Sir John Macdonald, embarked upon the National Policy—a policy ostentatiously protective. The later history of the tariff under the National Policy is shewn to be characterized by efforts more or less continuous to remove the crudities and inequalities of the earlier phases of the tariff and by efforts to modify those imposts which, while protecting one class of manufacturers seemed to injure others.

The oscillations between the policy of imposing specific and that of imposing *ad valorem* duties are very interesting to follow in detail, as also the tendencies to increase duties upon spirits and upon some luxuries on grounds partly economical and partly ethical.

The history of the Canadian tariff on its legislative side having been competently summarized, there remains the more difficult task of examining the course of prices in Canada, alike of manufactured goods and of agricultural products and of estimating the effect of tariff changes upon those prices.

The complex relations between tariffs and prices may probably form the subject of a similar study in the future.

JAMES MAVOR.

THE TARIFF HISTORY OF CANADA.‖

، I.

CONDITIONS PRIOR TO CONFEDERATION.

Prior to 1867 the provinces were isolated units and the amount of inter-colonial intercourse and commerce was but small. Each province went on its own way in matters pertaining to tariff legislation, endeavoring to secure its own immediate interests ; " each province did what was best for its own immediate wants, built its little Chinese wall around its own frontier and taxed the manufactures of a sister province as readily as those of Russia or the United States."* The inevitable results of this pursuit of individual provincial interests, were conflicts of tariffs and constant hampering of trade.

In Nova Scotia the general tariff rate was 10 per cent.† Although some favor is shown in this tariff to the manufacturers by the inclusion 'in the free list of materials suitable for manufacture, yet on the whole the revenue idea is the strongest. The semi-dependence of Nova Scotia on other regions for its supplies of agricultural produce is indicated by the placing of this on the free list. The tariff is characterized by simplicity—its duties are either *ad valorem* or specific, no place being found for compound duties. The fact that so many of the duties imposed are specific shows the somewhat crude nature of this tariff ; for specific duties, more especially in countries which have not reached a high state of commercial development, have a tendency to be applied in a rough and ready manner. Under a fixed specific duty the result is often inequitable ; for the proportion of duty-charge bears much more heavily on the poorer goods, and thus the poorer classes of the community, who consume these goods, are placed at a disadvantage. The *ad valorem* duties comprise three schedules, viz.: 20 per cent., 15 per cent., and 5 per cent. The 20 per cent. rate is imposed on luxuries and the finer classes of manufactured goods.

Although, in general outline, the tariff of New Brunswick‡ bears much resemblance to that of Nova Scotia, yet in one particular there is a difference. In the Nova Scotian tariff the free list had been made use of in order to extend inducements to manufacturers ; but in the tariff of New Brunswick this feature is absent. The general rate, indeed, is heavier, but the difference in rate is attributable to a greater need for revenue. Here, as in the Nova Scotian tariff, the specific rate of charge is favored. Luxuries, together with most of the commodities in common use, have a specific duty imposed upon them. In the case of wine there is a compound duty.§ This is a departure from the usual practice of these early tariffs for, in general, simple duties were preferred. The *ad valorem* goods

---

*Gray's History of Confederation, vol. 1, p. 12.

†Cap. 8, Revised Statutes of Nova Scotia, 1864.

‡22 Vict. N.B. 1859.

§2s, 6d. and 12½ per cent.

‖ The skilled and kindly advice and criticism of Professor Mavor have been of material aid to me in the revision of my essay. It affords me much pleasure to acknowledge my indebtedness to him.—S. J. McL.

8

are arranged in two lists, viz.: ship supplies on which there is a charge of 1 per cent., and machinery and iron manufactures which are taxed 15 per cent. The general rate on goods N. E. S. is 12½ per cent.*

In Prince Edward Island the tariff rate, at this time, was about 11 per cent.; while in Newfoundland it was on the average 10 per cent.†

The tariff of the province of Old Canada was the outcome of special circumstances; on account of the inland position of the province, and the greater charges incurred in the building of public works, and general internal development, it was found necessary to impose rates of duty heavier than those imposed by the provinces by the sea. In these earlier days the means of internal taxation were practically in their infancy, and hence the Government was forced to rely in great degree upon the customs duties. The two Acts of Old Canada which are of importance in this connection are those of 1859‡ and 1866.§ The latter, however, is the Act which outlined the tariff of the new Dominion, and may, therefore, be more advantageously considered in another connection.

Although the general rate on goods N. O. P. was 20 per cent., the duty in the case of specified commodities was, in many instances, much higher. The rates of charge vary from 100 per cent. in the case of liquors, to 10 per cent., in the case of iron and steel and their manufactures. The rate of duty on luxuries and quasi-luxuries is, in general, high. An attempt is made, however, to accommodate the tax to the different qualities of the commodity; for instance, there is a tax on sugars according to quality, of from 10 per cent. to 40 per cent. The tax on liquors is exceedingly high; in the tariff legislation of Canada, as in that of most civilized countries, there appears, on the whole, a uniform tendency to increase the duties on spirits, but this rate of 1859 was high beyond precedent. The reasons which led to the adoption of this rate were partly economic and partly ethical. The Finance Minister had proposed, in the tariff resolutions, a 50 per cent. tax**; but it was represented to him that such a "low rate of duty would encourage intemperance," hence the increased duty.†† The question of extending protection to mineral products was not considered in this tariff, for we find that lead, copper and iron ores were admitted free of duty. This serves to indicate the undeveloped condition of the mining industry.

The Canadian tariff differed from the Maritime tariffs in general principle as well as in more detailed outline. It has been shown that the Maritime tariffs were for the most part specific, the ad valorem system of duties holding only a subsidiary place. In the Canadian tariff the conditions are altogether different, for, with a few minor exceptions, the duties are ad valorem. The principle of substituting ad valorem for specific duties had been adopted when a new administration was formed in 1858; the change was advocated because it was considered that it would ensure a more equitable pressure of customs duties upon all. The proposed reconstruction of the tariff on an ad valorem basis was outlined in the

*The customs contraction N. E. S. signifies "not elsewhere specified,"; N. O. P. means "not otherwise provided for."
†Confederation Debates, p. 141. Speech of Hon. D'Arcy McGee.
‡22 Vict., Cap. 2.
§29-30 Vict., Cap. 6.
‖Bastable Public Finance, pp. 495-9.
**The 50 per cent. rate had been thought of because a similar rate was proposed in the amended tariff of the United States. The significance of this and similar facts will be considered in the Appendix. See "The Influence exerted upon the Canadian Tariff by the Tariff of the United States."
††Budget Speech, March 7th, 1859.

Speech from the Throne, and despite sundry objections that it would prove prejudicial to the interests of Upper Canada,* which imported more extensively than Lower Canada, the new tariff was carried into effect. The rates in this tariff† are much higher than those in vogue in the Maritime provinces. The years 1857-8 had been somewhat disastrous in financial circles, and the Canadian Government, finding itself much straitened for revenue, was forced to raise the tariff; an Act of 1858 had increased the general rate to 15 per cent.; in 1859 it was still further increased to 20 per cent. But there was also an avowed protective intent present in the tariff. When the tariff Acts of 1858-9 were passed the Colonial Secretary, the Duke of Newcastle, protested against the protective features of this legislation, but the Finance Minister asserted the right of the Canadas to conserve their own interests in the way they deemed best.‡ The tariff policy of Nova Scotia or New Brunswick affected directly only one province; the tariff policy of Canada affected two portions of country with divergent interests, and in the endeavor to accommodate these warring interests a protective policy was deemed to be of service. A brief tabular summary will serve to indicate the war of the tariffs. For this purpose the following commodities may be chosen: spirits, tea, sugars, tobaccos, agricultural products, iron and its manufactures.

—	Nova Scotia.	New Brunswick.	Canada.
Spirits	Specific, average rate 70c. per gallon	Specific, average rate 1s. 9d. per gallon...............	ad valorem 100 per cent.
Teas	ad valorem 10 per cent	Specific, 2d. per lb..........	ad valorem 5 per cent. to 15 per cent. according to quality.
Sugars	ad valorem 20 per cent	Specific, from $\frac{7}{10}$d. to 1½d. per lb. according to quality	ad valorem 10 per cent. to 40 per cent. according to quality and fineness.
Tobaccos	ad valorem 20 per cent	Specific, 2d. per lb ....'.....	ad valorem, mixed tobaccos 30 per cent, cigars 40 per cent.
Agricultural } products .. }	ad valorem, meat and poultry 10 per cent............	Free	Free.
....	other products free ...,....	....	....
Iron and its } manufact'r's. }	ad valorem 5 per cent	ad valorem 15 per cent	ad valorem 10 per cent.

That conflict of tariffs was one element in the plexus of causes which brought about Confederation is evident in contemporary speeches and newspapers. In the meetings of the delegates at Charlottetown "the detrimental way in which the conflicting tariffs operated to each other's disadvantage,"§ was referred to. The Hon. Geo. Brown, in a speech at the time, said: "but far in advance of all other advantages would be this that the union of all the provinces would break down all trade barriers between us and throw open at once to all a combined market of four millions of people."‖ The speeches of Cartier and other delegates were in the same strain. The position taken by the merchants is, however, more important in that it indicates the views of the mercantile classes, and here we find that the merchants and the delegates were at one. In the banquets which were

*Toronto Leader, January 31st, 1859, also re; ort, in Toronto Leader of March 16th, of meeting of Toronto Board of Trade.
†22 Vict., Cap. 2.
‡Budget Speech, 1859. See also Toronto Leader for March 12th, 1859.
§Gray's History of Confederation, vol. 1, p. 31.
‖Ibid, p. 42.

given to the delegates in Quebec much stress was laid, by Quebec merchants, on the fact that the doing away with hostile tariffs would be of much advantage to trade. At a banquet, given by the Quebec Board of Trade, Mr. Joseph* said : " we desire that the unequal and hostile tariffs of the several provinces should disappear, we want one tariff instead of five."† To allege that economic motives alone brought about Confederation would be to go too far; but none the less is it true that one immediate advantage that was expected from Confederation was a tariff which would forever do away with the constant friction that had hitherto existed.

It was necessary to obtain a uniform tariff. The Maritime delegates had been accustomed to a comparatively low rate of duties, and consequently they objected to the high tariff of Canada. One of the first things to be done then, before Confederation could become practicable, was the formulation of a tariff which should approximate to the lower rates of duties charged by the Maritime provinces.

II.

THE DAYS OF THE 15 PER CENT. TARIFF, 1867-74.

The delegates of the Maritime Provinces had made no secret of their dislike for the high tariff of Canada, and so an approximation to the Maritime tariff rate, which was on the average 12½ per cent., had to be effected. Accordingly the Tariff Act‡ which was passed was intended as a compromise. The duty rate on goods N. O. P. was reduced to 15 per cent., the general rate of the tariff of 1858 being thus accepted. As contrasted with the ante-Confederation tariffs, this tariff of the new Dominion bears the mark of compromise. Under the tariffs of the Maritime Provinces the duties had been for the most part specific ; under the Canadian tariff of 1859 the duties were, with one exception, *ad valorem* ; in the tariff of 1866 we find an attempt at a reconciliation of these divergent tendencies.

In addition to the specific duties in the new tariff we find three rates of *ad valorem* duties, viz.: 25, 15 and 10 per cent. The 25 per cent. schedule may be described as a tax on luxuries. The 15 per cent. schedule is the most important. It was from this list that the bulk of the revenue was expected, and it was from this list that the bulk of the revenue was obtained.

The influence of the sea-coast tariffs is seen in the substitution of specific for many of the *ad valorem* duties hitherto in force. Several instances of this may be cited. The Canadian duty on spirits had been an almost prohibitory *ad valorem* one ; the specific duty was now adopted,§ although the rate was somewhat higher than the average rates of the Maritime tariffs. Another instance is in the case of sugars where the *ad valorem* duty was also replaced by a specific rate,‖ the rate in this case also being higher than the corresponding one in the Maritime tariffs. In the Canadian tariff of 1859, as in that of New Brunswick, there had appeared isolated instances of compound duties. It can not be said that any real endeavor towards compound duties is manifested in the tariff of 1866, although there is a tentative attempt in this direction in the tax on tea**—an experiment.

*President of the Quebec Board of Trade.   †Gray, p. 83.   ‡29-30 Vict., Cap. 6.
§70c. to $1.20 per gallon.   ‖1.8c. to 3c. per pound.
**15 per cent. and ½c. per pound.

which was further followed out in the imposition of a compound duty* on tobacco
in 1867. There are fewer unenumerated goods in this tariff than in the earlier
tariffs. A case in point is the following: alcoholic perfumes had been included
in the general rate on spirituous liquors; now they are classed separately and
are made the subject of a specific tax.† This tendency, towards greater definiteness
in point of enumeration, comes as a consequence of the development of the tariff
and the more thorough acquaintance on the part of the legislature with the various
forms of taxable commodity.

The more definite adoption of the principle of protection is evidenced in the
free goods schedule, where, among other articles, are included colors, when imported
for the use of wall paper manufacturers.

Under Schedule F provision is made for reciprocal trade with the United
States in agricultural products, fish and lumber.

Although this tariff is to a certain extent the creature of opportunism and
compromise, yet, perhaps, it may be well to seek in it for some dominant principle. It has been argued by the Hon. Mr. Gray that, despite a temporary concession to protection in 1870,‡ this tariff was throughout a revenue one. The
dictum of one of " the Fathers " is of importance, but it may be possible to discover in the tariff itself, as well as in the views of those who had to do with its
enforcement, some conclusions that run counter to such a plea.

We shall first examine the internal evidence. It has been noted that the
25 per cent. schedule is practically a luxury tax. This tax may be looked upon
as a relic of the old idea that taxes should press most heavily on articles of
luxury. The evidence of history warrants the conclusion that taxes partaking of
the nature of sumptuary legislation are not highly successful, either in accom-
plishing their more immediate intention or in the secondary and more prosaic one
of raising revenue. The more specialized evidence of financial history also affords
evidence of the truth of this.§ The reason of this is not far to seek. The Finance
Minister has primarily to consider the question of raising revenue—although the
matter of incidence has also to be borne in mind—and he finds that, unfortu-
nately, it is the necessities of life which, under normal conditions, furnish the
bulk of the revenue. Luxuries are of fluctuating demand ; the demand for the
necessaries of life is less subject to change. The facts of Canadian financial history
show that the receipts from the 25 per cent. list were but small. Apart from
mere abstract questions of finance the discussion of this subject is of importance
in that it throws some light on the intentions of the framers of the tariff. The
ethico-economic views shown in this attempted control of luxury result from the
paternalistic conceptions which are associated with the theory of protection.

Another part of the internal evidence is to be found in the free list and
Schedule F. The free list states that iron, when in partial manufacture, is
admitted free, the intention being to benefit Canadian iron manufacturers. A
still more important clause in the free list is "colors, when imported for the
use of wall paper manufacturers—ultramarine, umber, blue-black, Paris green,
sugar of lead, etc.," shall be admitted free. There is here evident a desire to
benefit the home manufacturer by means of the free list. The provision made
for reciprocity with the United States is in itself an evidence of protective
intent, for such quid pro quo transactions are as a rule protective.

5 per cent. and 15c. per pound.
†$1.20 per gallon.
‡By the imposition of duties on breadstuffs and coal.
§Bastable's Public Finance, pp. 440 and 443.

Now with regard to the external evidence, this is to be found in the speeches of the finance ministers of the period 1867-74,* who, when more protection was demanded, or when the Government did not see fit to remit duties, defended the position taken on the ground that the tariff in vogue had protection in its nature, that in short it was a *national policy.*

Discrimination between " protection " and " incidental protection " is at best a vain one, for all do not see eye to eye on this question, there being no fixed standards by which the lines of demarcation may be determined. Sufficient, however, has been adduced, both of internal and external evidence, to show that somewhat of protection was present in this tariff. True, it was not protection in as high degree as afterwards appeared, but none the less was it protection. One cannot well leave out of consideration the free list and claim that because the duties are not on the face of them highly protective, therefore the tariff is not protective. As it affects a particular industry the effects are, in the main, somewhat similar whether a tax is imposed to benefit a growing industry or whether a tax is remitted to enhance its development ;† if articles used in further manufacture are placed on the free list the home manufacturer receives an advantage.

It was found necessary to insert in the British North America Act several sections dealing with the question of customs duties. It is provided‡ that the customs duties of the " different provinces shall remain in force until altered by the Parliament of Canada." It may readily be understood that this was simply a temporary expedient intended to tide over the intervening time until the Dominion Parliament should meet. When Parliament met representations were made by the Committee of Ways and Means which were incorporated in the Tariff Act of the year.§ The section which has specially to do with this matter is section 19—" So much of any Act of the Legislature of the late Province of Canada or of either of the Provinces of Nova Scotia or New Brunswick as imposes any duty of customs or makes any provision in any matter provided for by this Act or is inconsistent with this Act is hereby repealed." Thus was a general tariff applied to Canada.

Although the Dominion Parliament had thus legislated and had put in force a general tariff it might, at first glance, seem that it had tacitly abnegated some of its sovereign power to levy customs dues, for we find‖ that the right of New Brunswick to levy export duties on logs is still preserved. This would appear a serious violation of the section of the Customs Act already quoted. The provision contained in the B. N. A. owes its presence to peculiar circumstances. The export tax, so-called, on logs was really analagous to cullers' dues; it had been imposed in the form of an export tax because of the difficulty experienced in collecting it in the form of stumpage duties.** The tax†† on logs continued in force until 1871. When the Washington Treaty was signed, in that year, it was found that the continuance of the duties would run counter to the treaty obligations

*See more especially *Hansard* for 1871.

†Of course, the disturbing effects of the imposition of a new tax will have to be remembered in limitation of this.

‡Article 122, B.N.A.

§31 Vict., Cap. 7.

‖B.N.A., Article 124.

**Vide Gray's History of Confederation, vol. I., p. 65.

††This export duty on logs is provided for in Chapter 15, Title 3, R. S. of N. B.

incurred, and the export duty was thus repealed and an Act* was passed providing for compensation to New Brunswick.

The Customs Act which had been passed in 1866 was adopted in 1867 by the first Parliament of the Dominion. Two Acts were passed on the subject : the first† defining in greater degree the dutiable forms of spirits ; the second‡ imposing the new tariff. Section 19, already quoted, imposed, subject to Article 124 of the B.N.A., a general tariff upon the Dominion. One or two minor changes are made in this Act as compared with that of 1866. The Tariff Act of 1866 imposed a compound duty of 7c. and 15 per cent. on tea. There is a differentiation, for on black tea there is imposed a duty of 3c. and 15 per cent., while on green tea there is a rate of 7c. and 15 per cent. On tobacco§ there is a tax of 15c. and 5 per cent. In the case of the compound duties imposed under this Act there are undoubtedly two elements present, 1st, the desire to prevent under-valuation, 2nd, the desire to obtain revenue, the latter being probably the more important. The policy of imposing such a heavy tax on tea, an article which, although ostensibly a luxury, is almost a necessity to the poorer classes, is open to question—especially when the rates on liquors were low. The clause of the British North America Act which reserved to New Brunswick the right to impose " export " duties on logs gave rise to a similar claim on the part of Ontario and Quebec ; and thus we find that in the recommendation from the Committee of Ways and Means a provision was made for a duty on logs, etc., when exported from Ontario and Quebec.‖ The same relative justification for the imposition of such duties did not exist, in this case, as in the case of New Brunswick, and so with the leave of the House the motion was dropped.

The changes of 1868 had to do with details. The specific list was altered in a few particulars—animals were added, while ales, beer and wine were moved to the compound list. The free list was also extended by a further enumeration of iron. Provision had been made by a prior Act** for an export duty on lumber, i.e., as regards the Dominion ; in this year the provision was enforced. The rates chosen varied from $1 in the case of pine to $2 per thousand in the case of oak logs.

In the previous session a tax of 10 per cent. on breadstuffs had been imposed ; this was found to work in a way detrimental to the interest of the Maritime Provinces and it was removed.††

By this time the Canadian tariff had been sufficiently long in operation to afford some statistics with regard to the pressure of customs duties. A comparison of the trade and navigation returns for the year 1868 with the returns contained in the sessional papers of later years, gives the following results. The duty on the total imports, both dutiable and free is 12 per cent.; on the dutiable goods alone the average rate is 20.22 per cent. In order to estimate the pressure of taxation, both specific and ad valorem, some details may be given. On molasses the rate of taxation was, on the average, 46.94 per cent.; on sugar of all kinds, on the average, 43.18 per cent.; on flour and meal, 8.53 per cent., and on iron, 15.01 per cent. From this it may be seen that the average rate of duty on breadstuffs was low.

The year 1869 was not distinguished by tariff changes. In the year 1870 advantage was taken of the power given in 1869.§§ to impose drawbacks. The

---

*36 Vict., Cap. 4.
‡31 Vict., Cap. 7.
‖The proposed rates were :
  Pine logs.................. $1 00 per M.
  Other logs.............. 50 "
          Railway ties............ ......3c. each.
. **31 Vict., Cap. 44.
§§31 Vict., Cap. 44, sec. 10.

†31 Vict., Cap. 6.
§Cigars excepted.

Shingles and stave bolts. $1 20 per cord.
Hop poles .... 60 per 100.

†† Vide Toronto Leader, of April 30th, 1868.

power thus conferred was made use of in an endeavor to increase the number of ships built for export ; in particular a drawback was allowed on iron used in the manufacture of composite ships for export.* This, in the earlier years of its working, was the main use made of this provision. Judged from the theoretic standpoint, drawbacks may be characterized as a " harking back " to mercantilism.† Their relative justification, so far as a particular nation is concerned, depends upon the estimation in which the export trade is held by that nation. Under protection the export trade is made much of.

The legislation on tariff questions, in 1870, bears marks of tentativeness and hesitancy—a tentativeness and hesitancy which is characteristic of the succeeding year. The Act placing animals on the specific list in 1868, is now repealed, and animals are again placed on the *ad valorem* list. In this year, as in 1871,‡ judging from the evidence of *Hansard* and the journals, the Government, instead of leading, was driven.§

The necessity for increased revenues brought about some tariff changes. The duty on spirits was increased from 70 to 88 cents per gallon. An increase was also made in the case of the duties on wheat, breadstuffs and coal. In these latter duties the desire for revenue is not the most important cause ; the motive cause was more probably the idea that by this means greater pressure could be brought to bear on the United States Government, so that more favorable terms could be obtained in the Washington treaty.

These modifications which have been spoken of had to do with internal changes in the Act ; section 11 of the Customs Act of this year|| may be said to have effected an external change. This section provides for an increase of ¾ per cent. on all the dutiable goods ; that is, the duty leviable on an article was to be increased by the addition thereto of 5 per cent. of the amount of duty previously imposed on said article. It might be held that this addition to the duties imposed by the general tariff is sufficient to constitute this year a new tariff epoch ; but as the increase of duty amounted to only ¾ per cent.—the duties now standing on goods N. O. P. at 15¾ per cent.—it is well to consider it as an integral portion of the 15 per cent. tariff ; the more so as the increase was of short duration. It was expected that, from the minor changes in the tariff and the ¾ per cent. increase, there would result an increase in the revenue of $575,000.

The retaliatory duties which had been imposed by the Government upon coal and breadstuffs were not welcome to the general community ; neither was the ¾ per cent. addition. The Board of Trade of Montreal, as well as other representatives of local interests, petitioned against these increases. The feeling which had been shown in the session of 1870, did not lessen in the session of 1871. All through thesession petitions and questions were directed at the Government ; the gist of the general demand was that the obnoxious duties, of the previous session, should be either reduced or repealed. To cite but one of the many petitions which were presented, it may be noted that on March 22nd. Hon. Mr. Workman presented a petition from the Montreal Corn Exchange against the grain and flour duties, setting forth " the propriety of throwing off the duties on the necessaries of life in order to render this country a cheaper one to live in."** The cross-firing on this question took up much of the session. During this discussion an expression was employed which is important in the later tariff history of Canada. , Against the pro-

---

* 33 Vict., Cap. 9, sec. 13.

† *Vide* article on Drawbacks in Palgrave's Dictionary of Political Economy. Vol. I.

‡ With reference to the duties on coal and breadstuffs.

§ The debates and journals of the years 1870-1 are somewhat unsatisfactory ; it is almost impossible to discover in them any well-defined principle of procedure with reference to the tariff.

|| 33 Vict., Cap. 19.

** Commons' Journals and Debates, 1871.

posal to remit the duties it was objected by the Finance Minister, Sir Francis Hincks, that the action of the Government in imposing these duties, was in accordance with the " *National Policy*."

But although the Government took this position, it was forced at length by the popular demand to remove the grain and flour duties together with the general increase in the tariff rate;* by this means a reduction of $1,500,000 in duties was effected. This remission of duties is spoken of by some as marking the beginning of the " new tariff," but the contention is open to objection.

Two other provisions in the Customs Act of this year† are worthy of note, in that they established precedents, which have been more or less followed ever since. Section 4 provides that upon the authorization of the Governor in Council " machinery, the like of which is not manufactured in Canada " may be admitted free. Section 3 provides that the Governor in Council may from time to time transfer to the free list, articles used in course of Canadian manufactures. The discretionary power of the Governor in Council, manifested in these sections instead of diminishing increases; the tariff Act of 1894 expressly states that the power exists unchanged and unimpaired.

In the year 1872 the changes made had to do with the duties on tea and coffee. It was not so much the advisability of lightening the pressure of taxation, that influenced the Government, as the fact that it was forced into such a line of action by the tariff legislation of the United States. It may seem disingenuous to take such a view of the Government's action, but the words of Sir Francis Hincks hardly admit of any other construction being placed upon them.‡ He said in substance on May 21st, 1872 "that it was expedient that all the duties of customs whether *ad valorem* or specific now payable on tea and coffee should be repealed on and after July 1st next. . . . This was caused by the revision of the American tariff; it would be impossible for the Government to guard against American tea on the frontier." This reduction was accepted and embodied in statutory form.§

In this session the Canadian tariff was extended to British Columbia;‖ this was an evidence of the national growth and showed how the national power was being extended, for the tariff of the Dominion is but emblematic of the power of the Dominion. The year 1873 witnessed a further extension of the territory over which the national tariff had force, for in this year it was provided that on and after the 17th of May, 1873, there should be the same customs duties for Manitoba as for the rest of the Dominion.**

The year 1873 is the end of this period. In this the last year of the operation of the old tariff the duties remained at their normal level Some changes were made in the duties on ale, sugar and tobacco. These changes indicate a further taking into favor of the principle of compound duties. The policy with reference to the iron industry remains unchanged, the same encouragement being extended as heretofore; *i. e.* the iron goods on the free list are in a less advanced state of manufacture than those on the five per cent. list.

ʹ   During this whole period the duty on goods N. E. S. was 15 per cent.†† But in order to appreciate the pressure of duties on all dutiable goods, whether under specific or *ad valorem* rates, the returns of the Department of Customs must be referred to.‡‡ During the years 1868-74, a period of seven years inclusive, the average rate of duty on all *dutiable* goods was 19.50 per cent.

* 34 Vict., Cap. 10.   † *Ibid.*

‡ *Vide Hansard* and Journals of House of Commons for 1872.

§ 35 Vict., Cap. 11.   This effected a reduction in duties of $1,209,166.00.

‖ 35 Vict., Cap. 37.   ** 36 Vict., Cap. 39.

†† The ½ per cent. increase was but temporary.   ‡‡ Sessional Papers, 1893, Table I.

III.

THE 17½ PER CENT TARIFF, 1874-78.

TARIFF "FOR REVENUE ONLY."

The results of the stormy politics of 1873 were the substitution of a Liberal administration for a Conservative one; and the beginning of a new epoch of tariff policy. The period 1874-78 was one of difficulty in financial circles. The world-wide depression had its influence in Canada. So closely bound together are the nations that constitute the "Republic of Commerce," that the panic and depression which affect one section of the world, affect also all other parts of the commercial community. Such conditions as these made the task of the Finance Minister a difficult one. Whatever the ability of a financier may be, the effects of a long-continued depression, which reduces the volume of trade and so lessens the means for the raising of revenue, must of necessity, give rise to conditions, the control of which is, in great degree, beyond his power.

The policy now adopted was avowedly one "for revenue only." The new administration had paid much attention to the free trade arguments of Cobden and Bright, and had before its eyes as a conscious ideal the example of England. *Doctrinaire* adherence to a policy which should issue in free trade coupled with the depression that prevailed did much to bring about the subsequent downfall of the Ministry; for, at the time when the Government was devoted to free trade, there was also a popular demand for protection.

The general rate of duty was fixed at 17½ per cent; this was an advance of 2½ per cent. on the general rate of the former tariff. But it was not so much the increase as the purpose underlying it that agitated the popular mind. On the whole, during this period there was a slight increase in taxation. In the period 1868-74 the average rate imposed had been 19.50 per cent.; under the tariff of 1874-78 the average rate of duty was 20.456 per cent. Thus it can be seen that the pressure of taxation was but slightly increased; the way in which it was increased and the principle that actuated such increase is to be found in the tariff itself.

The Tariff Act of 1874* was passed in amendment of the Tariff Acts previously in force. The tax divisions of the old tariff were in the main retained. The 15 per cent. list was changed to 17½ per cent.† and a 20 per cent. list was also added. The 17½ per cent. list was intended to contain the articles with which the home manufactures came into competition—to this extent there was incidental protection.

Before dealing in fuller detail with the items of the tariff, it may be well to show from the statistical returns for the year, the relative importance of the different rates of duty and also the prior importance of the 17½ per cent. duty. The total amount of duty obtained in this year is divided as follows:

Total specific duty		$2,636,944 67
" compound duty		2,328,663 38
" 25 per cent. duty		282,676 56
" 17½ "		9,519,668 61
" 10 "		283,242 95
" 5 "		292,834 28

---

*37 Vict., Cap. 6.

†In this connection it is worthy of remark that the recommendation from the Committee of Ways and Means—*vide* Journals of House—reads: "All goods N. O. P. . . . . shall be charged with 16¾ per cent.," while section 4 of the Customs Act reads, "All goods N. E. S. shall be liable to 17½ per cent."

The list of goods paying specific duties is about the same as that of the year 1873. One of the chief additions to the specific list is in the case of teas and coffees. On these the following specific duties are imposed : Tea, green or Japan, .04c. ; tea, black, .03c.; coffee, green, .02c.; coffee, roasted, .03c. The necessity of raising more revenue brought about this change ; it was strenuously opposed in committee. The constant tendency of the duties on tobaccos and spirits to increase is manifest here. Cigars are now taxed 70c. per pound ; spirits enumerated are taxed $1.00 per gallon, an increase of 12c., while on uncnumerated spirits there is an increase of 30c. per gallon. There is no very perceptible tendency to increase the number of goods paying compound duties. The duty on tobacco and snuff, which had hitherto been 15c. and 5 per cent., was now increased to 12½ per cent. and 25c., while the duty on sugar was fixed at 25 per cent. and 1½c. This latter item is an addition to the compound list.

To come now to the *ad valorem* list, in addition to the 25 per cent. list, there appears a 20 per cent. list which may be considered a complementary "luxury tax." The goods taxed under this new list are silks, satins, velvets, gold, silver or plated ware and fancy goods. To the 10 per cent. list are added locomotive engines and their parts, and machinery for mills and factories, which is not manufactured in Canada. This list also includes cattle, green fruit, seeds and vegetables. The protection formerly extended, by means of the free list, to partially manufactured forms of iron is now taken away and a 5 per cent. tax is imposed.

In the tenth section of the Act,[*] however, there appears a departure from the purely "Revenue Tariff" standpoint. The provision in question, viz.: "That the Governor in Council may admit free of duty, until 1875, machinery to be used in Canadian manufacture the like of which is not made in Canada," is undoubtedly, on the face of it, a concession to protection. This provision had first been enacted in 1871, and had since then continued in force. To appreciate its bearing, in the present Act, it must be read in connection with the 10 per cent. list, which provides for the imposition of a 10 per cent. duty on "machinery for mills and factories, the like of which is not manufactured in Canada." These sections being read together, it is apparent that the obvious intention was to afford the manufacturer an opportunity of accommodating himself to the altered conditions. The privilege had been in existence for some years, and hence the manufacturer had become habituated to such exemption from duty. The change in the tariff, in this particular, had to be gradual, otherwise it would tend to produce a dislocation of industry.

In the year 1875[†] the chief change, in the way of the remission of duty, is the repealing of the export duty on stave bolts and oak logs.

The year 1876 witnessed an increase in the expressed desire for protection. The discussion of this tendency towards protectionism, as manifested in the popular mind and in the expressions of the Parliamentary representatives, comes up more fittingly in connection with the tariff of 1879. Suffice it to say that during the years 1876-8 the debates in Parliament on the relative merits of Protection and Free Trade as policies for Canada, were more and more numerous.

The administration was much exercised over the continued depression ; and a committee was appointed to investigate the causes of the depression. Interesting as the depression is, from the standpoint of general financial history, it is still more interesting in the bearing that it had on the more specialized question of Canadian Tariff History. Under the tariff of 1874 more than half the revenue was raised from the 17½ per cent. list. The effects of the continued depression were seen in a reduction of the volume of trade. In the 17½ per cent. list alone there was, in the six months ending December, 1875, a decrease in the importa-

---

tions of $10,700,000.00; as a result of this there was in this period a decrease of $1,860,000.00 in the revenue obtained from the seventeen and a half per cents. Such a condition of trade, accounts, in great degree, for the deficit of the succeeding year.

Such being the condition of the revenue, some measure of amendment was urgently needed. Accordingly, in 1877, an Act was passed amending the customs duties.* Although it was found necessary to increase the revenue, the Government was evidently actuated by a conscientious desire to keep the burden of taxation from being unduly great. Thus we find that the petroleum duty, which had been 15c. per gallon, was reduced to 6c. per gallon. The evident intention being to lessen the pressure of taxation on what was now a necessity. This benefit was, however, minimized by an increase of two cents per pound in the tax on tea. This was intended to counterbalance the diminution in revenue from coal oil. The advisability of taxing so heavily another necessity is at best questionable. The tax on malt was increased to 2½ cents per pound. This would mean an increased tax of about 3 cents per gallon on beer.† The general taxes on spirits were not raised, and it might be suggested that, comparing the comparatively low level at which the spirit tax stood, viz., $1.00 per gallon on enumerated and $1.50 on unenumerated, with the rate at which spirits are now taxed, some increase in the spirit duties might have been attempted. In this way the necessity of increasing the tax on tea might have been avoided either in whole or in part.

As far as changes towards compound duties are concerned, there are but two, and one of these counterbalances the other. Cigars, which had hitherto been taxed at 70c. per pound, had now imposed on them a compound duty of 50c. and 25 per cent., while on imported ale, beer and porter the tax was made specific instead of compound.‡

Some additions were made to the 10 per cent. list and the 17½ per cent. list. To the latter were added cotton, silk and linen thread; these had been on the 10 per cent. list. Tubes and piping were taken from the free list and added to the 10 per cent. list.

The duties, thus increased, were intended to increase the revenue by $500,-000.00. Although these amendments gave an increase, they by no means solved the difficulty. The deficit for the year preceding was $1,901,000.00; it can readily be seen that, if the deficit were to be averted, and the evil effects of the depression overcome by tariff changes, then the amendments of this session were not sufficiently drastic.

The effects of the financial depression were still felt§ for the normal customs revenue had decreased by $3,000,000.00. The imports had decreased one-third in value. The reduction of imports, *per capita*, was from $35.25 to $25.50. Although the revenue was in this state yet there were some signs of bettering conditions, for, in the seven months ending February 10th, 1878, the revenue amounted to $13,434,235.00 as contrasted with $12,494,779.00 in the corresponding period of the preceding year, an increase of about a million.

However, although the effects of the depression were thus becoming mitigated, and although there is some reason to believe that under bettering conditions deficit legislation might not have been such an ever present spectre, the electorate determined in favor of a protective policy. The consequence of this was that, in 1878, the revenue tariff was doomed. The conditions which heralded in this change in public opinion are of sufficient importance to warrant their being dealt with at some length in a separate section.

---

*40 Vict., Cap. 11.   †This chiefly affected the excise.
‡This tax now stood : 10c. per gallon in bottles, etc.; 12c. per gallon in larger quantities.
§*Vide* Budget speech of 1878.

IV.

THE STEPS LEADING UP TO THE NATIONAL POLICY.

The tariff change in the year 1879 is one of especial interest in that it is a definite popular adoption by the Dominion of Canada of the policy of protection ; since then Canada has continued under the same policy.

Before discussing the policy itself, it will be well to look somewhat at the history of the origin and growth of the protectionist movement in Canada—a movement which culminated in the policy adopted in 1879. In order to trace this development it will be necessary to quote somewhat copiously from the debates of the House of Commons, and the newspaper files of the time. The petitions which were sent in during this period were many, and the ends aimed at were diverse.

Beginning with the year 1870 we find expressions with reference to protection. Hon. Mr. Currier* presented a petition from the Ottawa Board of Trade praying " that a duty be imposed on coal, salt and petroleum, and on all manufactures imported from the United States, and that a duty be imposed on all articles imported into Canada from the United States, the same as similar articles were charged there." The object aimed at in this petition was a composite one ; it aimed at both protection and retaliation. Mr. M. C. Cameron[1] presented a number of petitions from the farmers of Huron and Bruce praying for prctection to Canadian production and manufactures. Mr. Godin[2] asked for increased protection for Canadian tobacco—this to be obtained by means of the imposition of a higher rate of duty. A petition was also received[3] from the Montreal Board of Trade the purport of which was distinctly counter to that of the petition of the Ottawa Board of Trade. Mr. Magill presented[4] a number of petitions for protection of Canadian products.

In the session of 1871 petitions on the subject of protection were received— but these were all in favor of the remission of the protective duties on bread-stuffs and coal. Sir Francis Hincks opposed such remission, claiming, in the course of his argument, that the duties were necessary to a " National Policy." The use of the term "National Policy" on this occasion is perhaps the first appearance of this term. It shows that, even at this time, a more purely protective policy was commencing to meet with favor on the part of administrators.

In the session of 1872 the petitions for protection were continued. Petitions were received[5] from S. David and others applying for more protection in connection with the cigar industry. The member for Leeds and Grenville, during this session, moved that a committee " be appointed in order to consider the advisability of protecting the farmer, chiefly by a protective tariff on agricultural products coming in from the United States." Later on[6] a petition was received from the Council of Agriculture of Quebec, asking for " a reajdustment of the tariff so as to encourage the cultivation of sugar, beet root, tobacco and other useful plants . . . and also that a duty be imposed on foreign agricultural products."

*On February 28th.
1. On February 28th, 1870.   2. *Ibid.*
3. On March 11th.   4. On March 30th.
5. On April 24th, 1872.   6. On March 31st, 1873.

The financial depression which existed during the Mackenzie regime intensified the interest in protection, and it is during this period that we find it definitively accepted as a party policy. In 1876 when Hon. Mr. Cartwright had moved that the House go into Committee of Supply, Hon. Mr. Workman* moved in amendment "that the House deeply regrets to learn that the Government has not proposed a policy of protection . . . and that the large amount of capital now invested in industries, and their present depressed condition render such a policy necessary to restore them to a condition of prosperity." Sir John A. Macdonald also moved, during this session, an amendment on the same lines as that of Mr. Workman, but both amendments were defeated. In this year a committee, which had been appointed by the manufacturers to see to the conservation of their interests, reported that they were in favor of the existing 17½ per cent. tariff being replaced by a 20½ per cent. one.

During the session of 1877 discussions, with protection for a text, were numerous. Sir John A. Macdonald moved† " that the tariff should be adjusted so as to benefit the agricultural, mining and manufacturing interests of the Dominion." Mr. Wood also proposed that the general tariff rate be raised to 20 per cent. Both propositions were rejected.

In the year 1878 expressions in favor of protection were many, both in the House and outside. The Liberal Conservative Association of Ontario, meeting in Toronto, resolved‡ :

1. We are satisfied that the welfare of Canada requires the adoption of a national financial policy which by a judicious readjustment of the tariff will benefit and foster the agricultural, mining and manufacturing interests of the Dominion.

2. That no such readjustment will be satisfactory to the interests affected, or to the country, if adopted as a provisional means only to meet a temporary emergency, or to supply a temporary deficit, nor unless it is made and carried out as a National Policy.

3. That until reciprocity is established with our neighbors, Canada should move in the direction of a reciprocity of tariffs so far as the varied interests may demand.

In the House the matter was also dealt with. Sir John A. Macdonald moved,§ in amendment to the motion of the Finance Minister to go into committee, "That . . . this House is of opinion that the welfare of Canada requires the adoption of a National Policy which by a judicious readjustment of the tariff will benefit and foster the agriculture, the mining and other interests of the Dominion . . . and moving (as it ought to do) in the direction of reciprocity of tariff with our neighbors as far as the varied interests of Canada may demand, will greatly tend to procure for this country eventually a reciprocity of trade." This amendment was defeated. Various other recommendations were made, e.g., in favor of a protective duty on flour and wheat, in favor of a duty of 75 cents per ton on imported coal, but the voice of the House was against protection. Then came the general election, the way in which the popular vote pronounced is matter of history.

---

*A few years earlier the same gentleman had presented a petition praying for the remission of the duties on coal and breadstuffs ; his change of opinion now is but an expression of what was taking place in the nation.

†On March 2nd.

‡On January 15th, 1878. *Vide* Canadian Annual Register, 1879.

§On the 7th of March. *Vide Hansard.*

The foregoing indicates briefly how the current of opinion set towards protection during the years 1870-8, both in the proceedings of the House and in popular opinion throughout the country. These facts may now be placed in more systematized form. To sum up :

1. The desire for protection was general and popular.

2. The manufacturing interests and the farmers were desirous of protection.*

3. Protection had, as one main end, in the first place, the obtaining of reciprocity.

4. The Conservative party had a policy at hand, ready made ; for both the name, " National Policy," and the rate, 20 per cent., of duties had taken hold both of the House and of the country.

V.

THE 20 PER CENT. TARIFF, UNDER THE NATIONAL POLICY.†

The adoption of the National Policy marks the beginning of one of the most important epochs in Canadian tariff history. The protectionist leanings, evidenced in earlier tariffs, had not been so pronounced ; although the tariff of 1867-74, had been protectionist in sympathies, yet the duties had been kept at a comparatively low level owing to the known opposition of the Maritime Provinces to high rates. To have imposed a fully protective policy at the time, would have necessitated increased rates of duty, but, as the financiers of the time had the fear of the Maritime Provinces before their eyes, nothing of the kind was then attempted.

To attempt to trace changes in tariff policy to single concrete influences, is a hazardous experiment. It is probable, however, that the highly protectionist tariff of the United States had some influence in moulding popular opinion. It would be venturing further into the field of conjecture to assume that the " National Spirit " inculcated by List, had influence in connection with the National Policy. It is certain that the views of List had this in common with the principles of the National Policy, that much stress was laid upon the importance of the development of home manufacturers and the building up of the National idea.

Various reasons co-operated to give the National Policy a great vogue at the time. The policy of the Mackenzie administration had been eminently cautious, to some it seemed cautious to the verge of timidity. The difficulties in financial circles rendered the task of the administration especially hard, and the people became weary of the seeming lack of success of the " Revenue Tariff " policy. They wished for better times, they blamed the Government for not bringing them about. Then there is also in a new country a desire for quick development and rapid expansion, but the Government did not seem to be in sympathy with these aspirations. There was growing up in Canada a new national spirit ; the spirit of independence, which prompted Sir A. T. Galt, in 1858, to state that

*In earlier years it had been claimed that the Canadian farmer did not need protection. *Vide* the government organ, the Toronto *Leader* for May 2nd, 1868.

†In the note in the Appendix on " Protection *versus* Free Trade " there will be found an outline discussion, in the course of which some general propositions are considered in the light of Canadian experience.

Canada had a right to regulate the tariff in her own interests, was also present in an eminent degree in the tariff discussions of 1878-9. Then also, wider national sympathies were at work ; the national territories had been extended ; the great Northwest had been added ; and the people desired a policy which would rapidly develop all the varied interests of the Dominion. The National Policy was the crystallization of the national idea. Perhaps the people placed too much reliance upon legislative enactment, but the belief in such panaceas is widespread.

By the Customs Act of 1879* the new tariff was put in force, and all previous Acts running counter to the provisions of this Act were repealed. Much interest had been taken in the proposed changes, and consequently, when Sir Leonard Tilley made his Budget speech, in which the detailed changes were stated, the public interest was excited. The policy of the Government was, in general terms, stated by the Finance Minister to be " To select for a higher rate of duty those articles which are manufactured or can be manufactured in the country, and to have those that are neither made nor are likely to be made in the country at a lower rate." This is a frank statement of the policy of protection.

The Finance Minister stated that there had been a deficit of $500,000.00 in the previous year. It was necessary to receive an increased revenue of $2,000,-000.00, " and in arranging for the levying of the additional duties, he would ask the House to consider how it might be imposed so as to give protection to home industries."

In the duties there is a general increase. The somewhat elaborate scheduling arrangements which had hitherto been in vogue are departed from and a more simple system adopted. The system of arranging goods under certain headings, e.g., 25 per cent., 17½ per cent., 10 per cent., etc., is now given up and many differing standards are chosen. The tendency towards compound duties is now more marked. Under the " Revenue Tariff" the duty on goods N. O. P., had been 17½ per cent. ; under the new tariff it was fixed at 20 per cent. However, the real weight of customs taxation is not evident from this alone ; the total duty, specific, compound and ad valorem, must be looked at in order to show what the real pressure was. It will be found more practicable to take, at a later time, the duty for the first five years of the new tariff's history and compare it with the rates of duty under the old tariff ; in this way the change in the rates may be more readily appreciated.

Specific duties, which had been but sparingly used in the old tariff, are now employed in greater degree.

To cite the tariff changes in detail would demand too much space. It will be sufficient to choose some items ; in this way the general spirit, which actuated the tariff, may be as well gathered as if more copious citation were indulged in. On two hundred and forty-five dutiable articles the average ad valorem duty was 22.26 per cent. ; in addition to this there is, on some of these articles, a specific duty. On agricultural implements the duty was now fixed at 25 per cent. On breadstuffs protective duties were imposed. In 1878 the breadstuff duties had been imposed in order to obtain better terms from the Americans ; now the duties were imposed in order to protect the Canadian farmer ; these duties on the main breadstuffs are as follows :

Barley, 15 cents per bushel ; buckwheat, 10 cents per bushel ; Indian corn, 7½ cents per bushel ; oats, 10 cents per bushel ; rice, 1 cent per pound ; rye, 10 cents per bushel ; wheat, 15 cents per bushel ; peas, 10 cents per bushel ; beans, 15 cents per bushel ; buckwheat flour, ¼ cent per pound ; cornmeal, 40 cents per barrel ; oatmeal, ½ cent per pound ; rice and sago flour, 2 cents per pound.

---

*42 Vict. Cap. 15.

On oatmeal, rice and sago the duties were comparatively high ; the duty on oatmeal was equal to about 20.63 per cent., while that on rice and sago flour is nearly 50 per cent. Under the former prices of wheat the duty rate in 1879 would be about 15 per cent.

On coal, both bituminous and anthracite, a duty of 50 cents per ton was imposed. On cottons, when unmade, there was a compound duty of 3 cents and 15 per cent.; when made up there was an *ad valorem* duty which amounted, on the average, to 17.91 per cent. With reference to the iron industry, although the rates are somewhat higher than formerly, it cannot be said that the duty was strongly protective. So far as avowed intention of fostering the iron industry by means of protective duties is concerned, the adoption of protection dates from 1887. Under the tariff of 1879 there are some thirty-six articles of iron enumerated in the taxing schedule. On some of these the duties are specific, on some compound, but taken as a whole there is an average, duty of 16.17 per cent., a slight increase as compared with the former rate of duty. Of sugar and molasses there are some twelve enumerations, seven of the forms so enumerated bear a compound duty. The average *ad valorem* duty imposed is 26.25 per cent. In the case of wool and woollen manufacturers the compound duty is favored. However, when the articles are imported to aid in further manufacture, there are only *ad valorem* duties imposed. The average duty on woollens was about 18 57 per cent. At the time an objection was made to the new taxes on woollens ; it was claimed that the pressure of taxation on the poorer qualities of woollens, used by the poorer classes, would be about 30 per cent. The highest *ad valorem* duty present is in the case of patent medicines, which are taxed 50 per cent.

Tobaccos are charged with a compound duty. The duties on spirits are for the most part specific ; although in the case of wines and cologne a compound duty is imposed. In the case of cologne the *ad valorem* rate is 40 per cent. The free list contains some 226 articles. There is an evident intention, in the use made of it, to further the development of Canadian manufactures. Thus the increased rates of duty and the free list are complementary elements in the protective policy. The power of the Governor-in-Council to transfer dutiable goods to the free list is still recognized.

The policy of allowing drawbacks which had been sanctioned in earlier Acts,[1] again received Parliamentary sanction ; for, in this year, it was proposed that a drawback, on the duties paid upon all articles entering into the manufacture of exported Canadian goods, should be allowed. In order to foster the shipbuilding industry, a drawback was also to be allowed in the duty paid on all articles entering into the construction of vessels for export.

The principle of imposing retaliatory duties on teas and coffees imported from the United States was still retained ; for in this session a duty of 10 per cent. was imposed on teas so imported.

One statement in the Budget Speech is significant, and that is with reference to the intentions of the Government towards the United States. One leading argument in favor of the National Policy had been that it would place Canada in a position of advantage with reference to the United States, so that thereby reciprocal trade privileges might be obtained. The Tariff Act of this year provided that, with reference to the natural products of both countries[2] if the United States repealed their duties, in whole or in part, the Canadian Government was prepared to meet them with equal concessions. Although the Government thus made a statutory offer of reciprocity, it had tired of the pacific attempts which had been used in the past. It is therefore of importance

---

1. 32 Vict. Cap. 4, Sec. 10.   2. Including lumber.

to note that the Finance Minister said that with reference to the United States, "the Government intended to impose duties on a great many articles imported from there which had been left on the free list since 1875 in the vain hope of inducing our neighbors to renew the Reciprocity Treaty." This intention is seen in the fact that the average duty on American goods under this tariff was 25 per cent.

The theory of the balance of trade was employed to justify, on economic grounds, the National Policy. Sir Leonard Tilley seemed ever to have present with him as one of his financial maxims the idea that an adverse balance of trade should be overcome. He seemed to believe that a favorable balance of trade was the end of all tariff legislation. In his Budget Speech in 1879, he stated his conviction "that the large balance of trade against us ever since Confederation was one of the main causes of our difficulties." In 1885, in making a comparison between the excess of imports over exports during the period, 1874-79, as contrasted with the excess in the period 1879-84, he pointed out that during the former period the excess had been $105,111,076.00, while during the latter period it had been only $82,059,368.00 ; he then said " as to the balance of trade I give the figures to show that the N.P. had the practical effect of keeping the difference between the imports and exports in a much more favorable condition than than it would otherwise have been."[1] It is evident from this that he thought that one main advantage of the National Policy was that it tended to bring about a favorable balance of trade.[2]

The general effect of the amendments which were made in 1880[3] was to increase the duty ; for example, on eight articles, including demijohns, artificial feathers, billiard tables, organs, pianos, slates, trunks and watches, there is an average increase of $5\frac{5}{8}$ per cent. In the case of pianos and organs a 15 per cent. *ad valorem* duty is imposed instead of a 10 per cent. duty as formerly ; the specific duty imposed on these articles remained unchanged. In the case of porcelain china there is a reduction of 3 per cent. The duties are increased on certain medicinal articles, *e.g.*, liquorice and liquorice root.

In the specific duties a tendency towards increased rates is also to be noted. For example, the duty on green fruit is increased from 1c. to 2c. ; on grindstones from $1.50 to $2 per ton ; while on tobacco the duty is increased from 50c. to 60c. per pound, the *ad valorem* duty remaining at 20 per cent. The changes in the free list do not appear to be made on any fixed principle.

Two other increases in duty may be noted by themselves. The Act of this year provides for a duty on cans containing fish, under the Washington.Treaty, of 1½ cents per quart can. The reason for this change is as follows: "It was intended to counteract the effect of American legislation by which the trade of the United States had an advantage over our people of 18 cents per dozen on all canned fish."[4] Such action may have been demanded in the interests of self-protection ; but the free entry of the contents of the can while the can itself was taxed may, with a show of reason, be considered as an observance of the letter but a violation of the spirit. The other noteworthy instance of an increase is in the case of coal. Coal, both bituminous and anthracite, which had been taxed 50 cents per ton under the Act of 1879, now had the duty increased to 60 cents per ton. This tax illustrates well the peculiar conflicts and complicating tendencies of local interests under a protective system, as well as the large amount of supervision which is necessary. The explanation given in the House with reference

---

1. See Budget Speech.

2. In the note in the appendix on "Protection *versus* Free Trade," there will be found a short discussion of the Balance of Trade Theory, more especially with reference to the result of the attempt to apply the theory in actual practice in Canada.

3. 43 Vict., Cap. 8.   4. Budget Speech for 1880.

to this tax was " that the increase of 10 cents per ton on coal, as compared with the 50 cents at which it had stood before, was imposed with the idea that this would carry Nova Scotia coal as far west as Hamilton; at 50 cents per ton it had gone as far west as Toronto."[1]

In 1881 the Tariff was still further amended.[2] Some explanatory changes were made. The Free Trade List was extended by the inclusion, among other articles of beans used in the manufacture of flavoring extracts, medicinal roots, and oak bark extract for use in tanning.

In Schedule A some changes are made. Breadstuffs when damaged in transit are now taxed 20 per cent. All the goods now added to Schedule A have an *ad valorem* duty upon them except checked winceys, which are taxed 2c. and 15 per cent. The tendency towards differentiation in enumerated goods is apparent in the provision that while winceys are charged with an *ad valorem* duty of 20 per cent., checked winceys pay a compound duty. Some eighteen articles chargeable with an ad valorem duty are included in the changes made. The duty varies from 5 per cent. in the case of paints, to 30 per cent. in the case of cartridges. The average *ad valorem* duty charged upon these eighteen articles is 21.94 per cent. The dutiable rate on spirits and strong waters varies from $1.32½ [3] to $1.90[4] per gallon. Sugars between No. 9 and No. 14 D.S.[5] are charged 1c. and 35 per cent.; below No. 9 D.S. ½c. and 30 per cent.[6]

In 1882 the Opposition attacked the duties on coal and breadstuffs, endeavoring, without success, to have them repealed. The amount of duty obtained from this source during the preceding year was $1,100,000.00. An Act [7] in amendment to prior customs acts was also passed in this year. By the Act of the previous year the period during which steel rails, fish plates, etc., could be imported free of duty had been extended; by this Act the period was still further extended.[8] In the enumerated articles of the tariff there were some eleven changes. In the case of six of these there was an average increase in the *ad valorem* rate of 5 per cent.; in one case there is a decrease.[9] In specific duties there is a decrease in the rates charged on iron; iron, old and scrap, being now taxed $1.00 instead of $2.00 per ton as formerly. The duties on spirits are increased and at the same time made compound.[10] The greatest increase in *ad valorem* rates is in the case of brass for printers' sticks, the duty being doubled.[11] In the case of cordovan leather where the duty is increased from 20 per cent. to 25 per cent., the intention is to extend increased protection to the manufacture of the finer grades of leather. On ship furnishings,[12] the following rates are imposed: on rigging 10 per cent., on machinery 25 per cent. It is to be remembered that a provision had been made for a drawback, in case these articles were imported to be used in the manufacture of ships intended for export. Some six formerly unenumerated articles are added to Schedule A; the average duty on five of these is 19.50 per cent. In the case

1. Budget Speech.
2. 44 Vict., Cap. 10.
3. In the case of gin, rum and whiskey.
4. In the case of essences, tinctures, etc.
5. Dutch Standard.
6. This is an increase as compared with the initial rate of the N.P.
7. 45 Vict. Cap. 6.
8. Until the end of the session of 1883.
9. Bookbinders' tools taxed 10 per cent instead of 15 per cent. as formerly.
10. The rate now standing at $1.90 and 20 per cent.
11. 30 per cent. substituted for 15 per cent.
12. From 1867-74 these had been on the free list.

of one of these articles, the precedent, of imposing a duty on cans containing free fish, is followed, for here there is a duty of 25 per cent. on bags containing free salt. The specific rates on fruit are increased. It was argued at the time that the fluctuating value of these articles rendered the specific duty preferable. It may be admitted that from the standpoint of the customs officer the specific duty was preferable, in that it facilitated his work ; however, the very fact that these articles were subject to sudden fluctuations in value rendered it all the more probable that the specific duty would entail an inequitable pressure upon the importer.

In the free list some twenty-two changes are made. The main tendency manifested is towards rendering free, articles which are of use in connection with mining processes, e.g. quicksilver and chlorides. A very important addition to the free list is the item which includes coffee and tea. In the case of coffee, however, the statute only provides for the free admission of green coffee. On tea—black, green and Japan—the duties were remitted. Thus the custom of the later period of the 15 per cent. tariff, was again followed. The retaliatory duty on teas imported from the United States was still retained.

The year 1883 saw still further changes in the Tariff. The Customs Acts were amended and consolidated,[1] and the duties were later on still further amended.[2] Although the National Policy had as one of the most important of its component elements the protective feature, yet the revenue element was of much importance. Of course the Tariff was not carried to the logical extent demanded by extreme protection, had it been so, it would have been destructive of revenue. The endeavor to protect Canadian industry had been made in a somewhat hurried and unsystematic way ; and this accounts for the fact that although a surplus of $4,460,000 had been counted on, the total surplus really amounted to $6,625,000.00. Thus, from the revenue standpoint, the Tariff had been even too successful. The fact that the estimates provided, in the first place, for so large a surplus as $4,000,000.00 was evidence of unskilful financing ; for close financing or even financing involving a small deficit is better for the country than a system which takes out of the pockets of the citizens a sum largely in excess of what is really needed.[3] The fact that the real surplus exceeded the estimated surplus by about $2,000,000.00 shows, in still stronger light, the crude financial legislation of the time. The Government was now confronted with the question what should be done with the surplus ; unless they desired to commit themselves to the Prussian " war-chest " policy, the only means available was to remit taxation. Accordingly taxation was remitted to the extent of $1,125,000.

In the amendments that were made it cannot be said that any well-defined principle is apparent. There is manifest a very slight tendency to increase the number of specifically dutiable articles. Playing cards which had been taxed 30 per cent. were now taxed 6c. per pack. In acids there is a slight increase of duty. A desire is evident to build up, in the country, the manufacture of railway cars, buggies, waggons, etc., for the duty on railway cars is now fixed at 30 per cent., while on buggies and waggons the rate is 35 per cent. In the case of manufactured tobacco and snuff there is a reduction of 5c. per pound, the duty now standing at 20c. and 12½ per cent. In the case of lubricating oils the tendency to differentiation, which is evidenced in the development of tariff legislation, is manifested. Hitherto all lubricating oils had been taxed 25 per cent. ; now the following division is made : Oil costing over 30 cents per gallon 25 per cent. ; oil costing under 30 cents per gallon 7 1-5 cents.

---

1. 46 Vict. Cap. 12.   2. 46 Vict. Cap. 13.

3. *Vide* Adams' Public Debts pp. 80-3.

In the dutiable list a number of changes are made; nineteen of these are *ad valorem*, and upon these there is an average duty of 21.44 per cent. On three items there is a specific duty imposed viz. : Jellies and jams 5c., vaseline 4c., and steel $5 per ton. As far as the items added to the dutiable list are concerned there is shown a slight tendency to favor the principle of *ad valorem* duties. The articles added illustrate the tendency still further to search out forms of taxable commodity. The duty on agricultural implements which had hitherto stood at 25 per cent. was now increased to 35 per cent. The rates of duties on minerals and their manufactures were also increased : for example, on iron pumps the duties are fixed at 35 per cent., on files and rasps at 35 per cent. This evidences the increased interest taken in the iron industry. It had been provided by the acts of previous years that steel ingots, bars, sheets and rails should be admitted free of duty for a time ; by the statute of this year this period was to end on July 1st, 1883. After this, steel, in the forms specified, is taxable with a duty of $5 per ton.[1] In the free list there are some 25 additions; these include iron, and copper wire, and beams.

On the whole it may be said that the Act of this year had but little effect on the Tariff. There are some slight reductions, as for instance, in the tax on manufactured tobacco and snuff which stands at 20c. and 12½ per cent., as contrasted with 25c. and 12½ per cent., which was the former duty. But such slight decreases are more than counter-balanced by increases on other lines of goods. A slight tendency to favor *ad valorem* duties is manifested; but additions are also made to the list of goods paying specific duties, as well as to those paying compound duties.

In an earlier part of this essay the intention was stated of making a comparison between the respective rates of duty under the " Revenue Tariff," and under the " National Policy." For this purpose the total amount of duty—specific, compound and *ad valorem*—during the " Revenue Tariff " period as well as the total amount of duty during the first five years of the " National Policy " has been collated from the statistical papers.[2] Then the total amount of goods entered for home consumption, less the amount of free goods has been taken, and the percentage of duty calculated thereon with the following results : •

REVENUE TARIFF PERIOD.

						Per cent.
During 1874	the rate of duty on all dutiable goods was on the average	19.32.
" 1875	"	"	"	"	19.53.
" 1876	"	"	"	"	21.30.
" 1877	"	"	"	"	20.63.
" 1878	"	"	"	"	21.60.
An average rate during this period of						20.456.

1879—1883.

						Per cent.
During 1879	the rate of duty on all dutiable goods was on the average	23.35.
" 1880	"	"	"	"	26.11.
" 1881	"	"	"	"	24.51.
" 1882	"	"	"	"	26.40.
" 1883	"	"	"	"	25.32.
An average rate during this period of						25.148.

1. Under the Act of 1879 it had been taxed at 10 per cent. *ad valorem*.
2. *Vide* Sessional Papers of 1893 and Statistical Year Book for 1892.

The difference is thus about 5 per cent. on the total. It is to be noticed that the full force of the National Policy did not commence to be felt until 1880. About that time the normal level of the duties during this period was reached. During the later periods of the operation of the tariff there has been an increase in the average rate and now that rate is nearer 30 per cent.

By the year 1884 the National Policy was well in hand, and its possibilities in the way of the production of reveuue were better understood. Although it was working more smoothly amendments were still found necessary and accordingly an Act on the subject was passed in this year.[1]

In the free list there are some twelve additions. These are mostly concerned with the iron industry. Although a specific duty of $5 per ton had been, during the last session, imposed on steel, in this Act iron and steel beams, sheets, plates, angles and knees were placed upon the free list. However, it is only when they are to be used in the construction of composite ships that they are to be so treated.[2] The obvious intention of this is to give an impetus to the ship-building industry.

Thirty changes are made in the dutiable list. In the case of acetic acid the rate is doubled.[3] Some changes are made in the cotton schedule : for instance, in the case of jeans and coutilles an *ad valorem* rate of 20⅔ per cent is substituted for the compound rate hitherto in force. The compound duty on cotton warp is reduced ; an *ad valorem* rate of 15 per cent being substituted for the compound rate which had hitherto obtained.[4] The most important change is in the rates on sugars. A change was made whereby a differential gain of 2½ per cent. was given to the direct importer ; the intention being to develop direct trade between the place of growth and Canada. The following tabular summary shows this differential advantage :

New rate when imported direct.	New rate when not imported direct.	Old rate.
Above 14 d. s............1c. and 32½ per cent..............	1c. and 35 per cent..	1n. and 35 per cent.
Between 9 and 14 d. s....⅔c. " 27½ "	⅔c. " 27½ "	⅔c. " 30 "
Below No. 9 d. s.........½c. " 27½ "	½c. " 30 "	½c. " 30 "

This duty has features in common with the duties imposed on teas imported from the United States. Throughout this Act the protective idea is strongly present, and such modifications as are made, as in the case of the sugar duties, are made with the intention of further developing Canadian trade by protective measures.

The act of 1885[5] also amended the Tariff. It is one of the awkward features of protection that the legislators' work, in connection with tariff modification, is never done. To the free list are added some twenty-six articles ; here again there is a further inclusion of steel and iron in the rougher forms, to be used in further manufacture.[6] On plate glass there is imposed what may be called

1. 47 Vict Caps., 29 and 30.
2. A drawback had been allowed before.
3. In 1881, the rate on acetic acid was 12c. per gallon ; now it was increased to 25c. per gallon.
4. The former rate was 3c. and 15 per cent.
5. 48-9 Vict Cap. 61.
6. *e. g.*, steel for skates, hoop iron for tubular rivets, and steel for shovels and spades.

a *differentiated* duty.[1]   The average rate on dutiable articles chargeable with an *ad valorem* rate under this Act is 23.8 per cent.   On the whole *ad valorem* duties are preferred to specific and compound.

The upward tendency of duties on tobaccos and spirits is also manifest ; on cigars and cigarettes a compound duty of $1.20 and 20 per cent. is imposed.[2]   On gin, rum and whiskey, etc., the rate is $1.75 per gallon, on brandy $2.00 per gallon.   In the matter, of the spirit duties, there is shown variable legislation.   In 1882 a compound duty had been imposed,[3] here we find the specific duty again taken into favor.   On tobacco and snuff there is an increase of 10 cents per pound.   The duties on fish are for the most part specific ; except in the case of fish oils and fish preserved in oils where the *ad valorem* duty averages 25 per cent.

In 1886 the control of the Tariff was under the hands of the new Finance Minister, Hon. Mr. McLellan.   The Act [4] of this year provides for further amendments of the already much amended Customs Act.   Some 63 changes are made in Schedule A : to judge by proportions specific duties were somewhat favored in this year for, in fourteen instances, specific duties are substituted for the duties hitherto in force.   Seven articles are taxed with a compound duty.   The average pressure of customs duties is somewhat higher than formerly ; as compared with the rates of the previous year the average duties stand 27.52 per cent. and 26.11 per cent. respectively.   In general the spirit duties are unchanged; in the case of cologne, however, the *ad valorem* duty is increased by 10 per cent.   The highest *ad valorem* duty imposed is in the case of colors which are taxed 53 per cent.   The course of action pursued with reference to two classes of articles is worthy of note ; these articles are iron and sugar.   In this year, as in the years that precede, there is evident a growing sense of the importance of the iron industry, and consequently attempts were made from time to time to manipulate the protective duties in such a way as to benefit the iron industry.   In the case of iron nuts, bolts, washers and rivets, the protective duty is increased and made compound.[5]   In the case of barbed wire there is a change from *ad valorem* to specific, the duty also being increased.   The rate on carriage hardware is increased by 5 per cent. ; on scythes there is also an increase in the specific duties.   In addition to this a bonus of $1.50 per ton on pig iron is provided for.[6]   In 1884 a new method of arrangements had been introduced in the sugar schedule, whereby a 2½ per cent. advantage had been given to the direct importer.   Now a change is made with the further intention of developing the refining industry.   It was provided that sugar under No. 14 Dutch Standard, when intended for refining purposes, should be taxed at 1 cent.   In sugars not intended for refining there are some changes e.g. sugar under No. 14 D.S., not for refining, is taxed at 1 cent and 30 per cent.—this is an increase of ¼ of a cent per pound ; sugars above No. 14 D.S. are taxed ½ a cent and 30 per cent.   On these two classes there is thus, over all, an increase of ¼ of a cent per pound.

Schedule C. of the Act of 1879 had provided for the free entry into Canada from Newfoundland of fish, fish oils and fish products.   This privilege had been abrogated by the Act of 1885, which contained a provision with reference to the duties on fish, fish oils and fish products.   The Act of this year also contains a

---

1. The duty varies from 6 to 9 cents per square foot according to the number of square feet in the sheet.
2. This is an increase of 60 cents per pound as contrasted with the rate of 1881.
3. $1.90 and 20 per cent.
4. 49 Vic. Cap. 37.
5. Before this it had been 30 per cent. *ad valorem*.
6. 49 Vic. Cap. 38.

provision with reference to this. In the matter of whale and fish oils there is a reduction in duty of 5 per cent. It is, however, provided, in the third section of the Act, that the fish and fish products both of Newfoundland and the United States may be imported into Canada on reciprocal terms.

In the export duties an increase of 50 cents per cord on shingle bolts and $1 per thousand on pine logs is made. Provision is also made for further increase, such increase being brought into existence on the discretion ot the Governor-in-Council. This discretionary power is granted in section 319 of the Tariff which reads, with reference to export duties "provided that the powers vested in the Governor-in-Council by section 97 of this Act shall extend and apply in all respects to the above named articles, and that the Governor may increase the export duties on pine logs to $3 per M."

Ever since confederation there had been contained in the different tariffs a schedule of prohibited goods ; the importation of such goods entailing upon the importer, by way of penalty, a heavy fine. These goods comprise in general terms, books, documents, etc., of a treasonable, seditious or immoral nature ; and counterfeit coin.[1] Somewhat of a departure in policy is now made, in that oleomargarine is included in the list of prohibited goods.By this means more protection was extended to the butter manufacturers. The protective nature thus becomes more noticeable in Schedule C. ; hitherto this feature had been absent in this schedule.

The years 1887-8 were characterized by an insistence upon one feature of the National Policy, to which, for some time, there had not been much attention paid. It will be remembered that the increased ability to obtain reciprocal trade with the United States was one of the advantages which, it was assumed, would be consequent upon the adoption of the National Policy. There had been made, in 1879, a statutory offer of reciprocity ; but the matter did not excite much interest. But now more attention was paid to the subject and reciprocity had a momentary popularity. The Tariff Amendment Act,[2] of 1887, made some very important changes.[3] The general effect of the changes made was in the direction of increasing the rate of duties. There is not manifested any marked preference for any one class of duties. The increased pressure of customs duties may be seen from the fact that the average rate during this year, was 30 per cent. as contrasted with 27.52 per cent. the preceding year.

In the somewhat complex arrangement of specific, *ad valorem* and compound duties on buggies and wagons, there is a conscientious endeavor to reach the various forms of taxable commodity.[4] But the specific tax being imposed on the lowest priced wagons and buggies ensured that while, from the standpoint of the tax gatherer, there was a moderate advantage, from the standpoint of the consumer there was a pronounced disadvantage. On some items of cotton, namely, jeans, coutilles, printed and dyed cottons, there is a general increase of 5 per

1. Since then "reprints of Canadian copyright works, and reprints of British copyright works which have been also copyrighted in Canada " have been added.

2. 50-1 Vic. Cap. 39.

3. From this year onwards the perusal of the Budget Speech is more advantageous to the student than hitherto. There is somewhat more of definite plan evident.

4The following is the arrangement:
   On those under $50.00 a specific duty of $10.00.
   On those between $50.00 and $100.00, $15.00 and 20 per cent.
   On those costing $100.00 and over, 35 per cent.

cent. On cigars and cigarettes the compound rate is increased, a rate of $2.00 and 25 per cent. being substituted for the former rate of $1.20 and 20 per cent. The protective features of these amendments affect the farming classes also. This may be seen in the following changes: on potatoes the former rate of 10 cents per bushel is replaced by a new rate of 15 cents; tomatoes are taxed at 30 cents and 10 per cent. in place of the old rate of 10 per cent.; on vegetables, in general, there is an increase of 3 per cent.

The changes with reference to the iron industry are the most important. In making these changes Sir Charles Tupper proceeded on the principle that the duties were to be proportioned to the amount of labor expended on the industry. The duties were based on the American duties on iron and steel, the proportion being two-thirds to one.* For a long time the free list had been utilized to enhance the growth of the Canadian iron industry; duties of varying magnitude had been imposed on various forms of iron; but the question of protection was subordinated to the question of revenue. It was in this year that the Government saw fit to devote more systematic attention to the development of the iron industry. If protection is beneficial, and if it should be extended to industries, then it logically follows that it should be extended to the important industry of iron. In England during the earlier period of the development of the iron industry a protective policy prevailed; it may safely be conceded that this policy had much to do with the development of the English iron industry; it would, however, be unsafe to suppose that to this phase of policy alone, is traceable the differential advantage which in, this particular, England possesses.

In the process of Tariff change there is often found at work not a simple motive but a complex series of motives. The imposition of increased duties on iron was entirely in accord with the dictates of protection, and the desire to develop the iron industry would of itself, have been sufficient justification, from the standpoint of protection, for the Government's action. But there was a political as well as an economic motive at work. The importance of Tariff conflict, as one of the causes which led to the formation of the Dominion, has already been indicated; once the Dominion was formed, the Tariff was, from time to time, used as an instrument to conciliate divergent interests. The Province of Nova Scotia had been reluctant to enter the federation and the magic of "better terms" had much to do with her entrance.† In 1879 the coal tax had been imposed to benefit Nova Scotia by securing the Canadian market to the Nova Scotian coal miner.‡ But still the dissatisfaction continued and, in the election of 1887, there was open discussion of the advisability of Nova Scotia seceding from the union. The iron interests of Nova Scotia were great and the increased rate of duties extended an especial protection to them. The Nova Scotian papers of the time recognized the change as in the nature of a concession to their Province, and the general impression was that the effect of the policy of the Government would be such that Nova Scotia would become "in the political system of Canada, what Pennsylvania is in the American union.§"

*See *Monetary Times* May 20th, 1887, and also Drummond's *The Iron Industry* pp. 23-24.
†See Toronto *Leader* for March 30th, 1868.
‡This had been proposed in 1867, but had not been enacted. See Toronto *Leader* for March 30th, 1868.
§See *Monetary Times* for May 20th, 1887.

The table given below includes the chief changes :

—	Rate of 1879.	Rate of 1887.
Pig iron	$2 per ton	$ 4 per ton.
Slabs, booms billets, etc	12½ per cent.	$ 9 "
Bars, rolled or hammered	17¾ "	$13 "
Railroad rails	15 "	$ 6 "
" fish plates	17½ "	$12 "
Band and hoop	12½ "	$13. "
Iron and steel wire	15 "	25 per cent. per ton.
Stoves, etc	25 "	$16 per ton but not less than 30 per cent.
Gas pipes, etc	25 "	$12 " 35 "
Car wheels and axles	25 "	$30 " 35 "
Rolled beams, channels, etc	15 "	½c. per lb. and 10 per cent.
Iron bridges and structural iron work	25 "	1¼c. per lb. but not less than 35 per cent.
Iron and steel forgings	20 "	1¼c " 35 "
Locomotives	25 "	30 per cent.; if over 3 tons shall pay specific duty of $2,000.
Drawn boiler tubing	10 "	15 per cent.
Skates	30 "	20c. per pair and 30 per cent.
Tinned and enamelled ware	25 "	30 per cent.
Builders' hardware	30 "	35 "
Bolts, rivets, etc	30 "	1½c. per lb and 30 per cent
Horseshoes and horseshoe nails	30 "	1¼c. per lb. but not less than 35 per cent.
Iron wire nails	30 "	1½c. " 35 "
Scales, balances, etc	30 "	35 per cent.
Nails and spikes (cut)	½c. per lb. and 10 per cent.	1c. per lb. and 25 per cent.
" (pressed)	½c. " "	1¼c. per lb. but not less than 35 per cent.
Adzes, hammers, etc	30 per cent	35 per cent.
Shovels and spades	30 "	35 "

When the iron rates of 1879 and 1887 are compared it is seen at once that the Tariff of 1879 was exceedingly simple in form. In 1887, however, the conditions are changed ; but few *ad valorem* duties appear, their place being taken by specific or compound duties. Some of the specific duties are simple, others are more complex and partake of what might be called a *quasi ad valorem* nature.* Under the Tariff Act of 1879 the general rate on iron and steel manufactures N. O. P. had been the same as the general tariff rate, namely, 20 per cent.; but in the Act of 1887 the general rate on iron and steel manufactures N. O. P. is 30 per cent. During the period, 1879-87, the average rate on iron and steel was 20.78 per cent. ; in the year preceding the revision the highest rate was reached, namely. 22.15 per cent. In order to compare with this the operation of the iron duties of 1887, the average pressure during 1888-93 may be taken. In 1887 the average rate of charge had been 22.15 per cent. ; in 1888 it at once rose to 30.06 per cent. ; from then to 1893 it fluctuated somewhat, but the normal rate throughout this period was 28.88 per cent. The average rate of 1887 is thus at least 8 per cent. higher than the average rate of 1879.†

The year 1888 is, in many ways, the complement of 1887. In this session the chief Tariff questions discussed centred around reciprocity and the export duties.‡

---

*E. g. such a duty as " 1½ cents per pound, but not less than 35 per cent."

†In the calculation of the average duties, the percentage of duty on the dutiable goods has been calculated. For dutiable goods and amounts of duty paid see the trade and navigation tables for the years in question.

‡51 Vict. Cap. 15.

From the beginning of the Canadian Tariffs the only commodity upon which an export duty had been imposed was timber, in its rougher forms. There was a popular opinion that it would be to the advantage of Canada to have the manufacture of this timber, into the finer grades, carried on in Canada rather than in another country. The foreign purchaser had been in the habit of manufacturing this timber, into the finer grades, in his own country ; it was supposed that the imposition of these duties would compel him to carry on the manufacture in Canada. These duties had not the anticipated effect. The amount of duty produced was not great, and the tax had had a prejudicial effect upon the Canadian timber trade. A feeling in favor of the abolition of these duties had commenced to manifest itself; and thus a resolution was passed in committee giving the Governor-General-in-Council power to reduce the duties "entirely or in part." Although power was given to reduce these duties, yet the Governor-General-in-Council* made use of the power conferred in terms of a prior statute† to increase the duty on pine logs to $3 per thousand. Such contradictory policy appears, on the face of it, somewhat strange. But it is probable that it was intended, by this action, to bring pressure to bear upon the United States Government, and so to ensure a more favorable hearing of the statutory proposals with reference to reciprocity contained in the Act of this year.‡ The provision, with reference to reciprocity, is, in the main, the same as that contained in the Act of 1879 ; there are, however, some minor differences. The Act of 1879 included trees, coal, coke, shrubs and wheat; these are not contained in the statutory offer of this year. But the offer of this year contains several items which are not included in the earlier Act, viz., wood pulp, stone or marble in the rough, fish oil and fish products. The most significant change in the statutory offer is in the omission of wheat.

No change of importance was made in 1889. During the session various questions with reference to the pork duties came up. The lessening of the duties on mess pork was asked for ; §but as the tariff had been amended so recently the Government did not see its way to further amend the tariff during this year.

---

*By Order-in-Council dated November 13th, 1888, (*Canada Gazette*, Vol. XXII., p. 860). The tax was again reduced by Order-in-Council of June 28th, 1889.

†Item 819, Schedule E, Cap. 33, R. S. C.

‡Section 9 in amendment of section 9 of 51 Vict. Cap. 15.

§This was dealt with in the Act of 1894. A duty of 25 per cent. was imposed on both mess pork and the lighter varieties. The effect of this was to increase the duty on mess pork and decrease it on the lighter kinds. The duty on the lighter kinds of pork had been 3c. per pound.

VI

THE BEGINNINGS OF TARIFF REFORM, 1890.

From 1890 onward there appears a more marked appreciation of the limitations of a system of protection ; but it is not to be imagined that the principle of protection is departed from, for, in some cases, the duties are actually raised ; yet the tendencies of the time, the attempts to combine the maximum of protection with the minimum of pressure, the choice of forms of duty whose pressure is supposed to be more equitable, the simplification in point of enumeration —are all indicative of a beginning of reform.   Then, in addition, there is a more defi.iite plan apparent.   Owing to the undue application of the protective principle in the earlier years, the National Policy disquieted the financiers by the presence of troublesome surpluses.   In process of time the application proceeded on a more definite plan ; and this is most markedly shown in the present period.[1]   Hitherto also, in the conferring of protection, it was, in the main, the producer who had been considered ; there is now a tendency to pay more attention to the consumer.

It might be argued that the reductions in taxation which took place in earlier years were indicative of the beginnings of a period of Tariff Reform—as fcr example the remission of the tea duty, or the placing of anthracite coal on the free list. These remissions, however, were spasmodic and did not proceed from a well defined plan of change.   Beginning with the year 1890, there appears a more adequate apperception of the fact that the tendency should be towards the minimizing of duties.   Although there exists, on the part of the Finance Department, this tendency towards systematization and gradual reduction of the Tariff Duties, it must be conceded that the reconciliation of the conflicting claims of differing industrial interests, has somewhat retarded the carrying into action of the plans of Tariff Reform formulated.

The year 1890 may be taken as the beginning of the period of Tariff Reform.   The Act of this year[2] provided for amendment in the Tariff.   It is not only in the Act itself but also in the statements of the Finance Minister that we have to look for the purpose that actuated the changes. [3]   In introducing the changes he took occasion to define the reasons that had caused the introduction of the Amendment Act.   He said that the purposes of the amendment were :

1. Explanatory—there had been confusion in the headings.

2. To reduce in some instances existing duties, which changed conditions have rendered higher than they should be, or duties upon articles which failing to be manufactured in this country should bear a Revenue Tariff and a Revenue Tariff only.

3. To put on the free list articles which either serve as raw materials for manufactures, or which would by their admission help to develop the resources of the country.

4. To readjust certain duties.

---

1. In the accomplishment of these changes much use is made of the free list.   It may be noted that the amount of free goods imported is steadily increasing—in 1893 it amounted to $52,000,000.00. (See Table I. in Appendix.)

2. 53 Vict., Cap. 20.

3 *Vide* Budget Speech of 1890.

It is evident from these resolutions that a belief in the protective principle is retained; it is none the less evident that a tendency towards modification has appeared.

In the Act itself, there are numerous changes. In the list of dutiable goods there are some 227 changes. In Schedule A the average *ad valorem* duty on 149 articles is 25.12 per cent.: on some of these articles the duty is compound. There are 65 articles on which there is either a specific duty alone or a compound duty. Changes are also made in the free list. The export duties on pine, oak, and spruce logs and shingle and stave bolts were removed by order in Council*—this change is a further evidence of the systematizing tendencies of the period; these duties had not effected the end for which they had been enacted.†

In virtue of the power to confer drawbacks, a drawback of 90 per cent. is allowed on imported Indian corn.‡ Spirituous liquors are charged on the average $1 per gallon; on six kinds of liquors there is in addition an average of 30 per cent. *ad valorem.* The chief liquors charged with a compound duty are those which are partly alcoholic in their nature, *e.g.*, elixirs, anodynes and alcoholic perfumes. In line with the policy adopted in 1887 some further protection is extended to iron and steel. On picks and mattocks the duty is fixed at 1 cent per pound and 25 per cent.—this is a duty of about 40 per cent.; on files and rasps 10 cents per dozen and 30 per cent.—on files this would give a duty of about 36.53 per cent, while on rasps it would be about 31.16 per cent. On shovels and spades the specific duties remain unchanged, while the *ad valorem* rate is increased 5 per cent. The fruit duties, as also the duties on hats, caps, gloves and mitts, are increased. There is a 10 per cent. increase on builders' and harness-maker's hardware. In these changes there is on the whole, a tendency to prefer *ad valorem* to specific duties.

In the year 1891 some important changes§ took place in the Tariff, chiefly with reference to sugars, spirits and tobacco. It has been seen, in the acts of previous years, that protective measures had been plentifully applied to the sugar industry. It had been attempted to increase the direct import trade, and later on the sugar refiner had been given an advantage. So far the pressure of taxation on sugar had been heavy; during the period of 1879-90 it had averaged 52.40 per cent.|| The change in duty which was now made was to the direct benefit of the consumer.

The taxes on raw sugar which had amounted to $3,500,000 per annum were remitted and the following provision was inserted in the free list, "all cane-sugar or beet-root sugar not above 14 D.S., in color; all sugar sweepings, and sugar drainings or pumpings drained in transit, all melado or concentrated melado, all molasses or concentrated molasses, N.O.P. all beet-root juice—when imported direct from country of growth and production." The idea of developing the direct trade at the expense of the indirect, was thus still retained. In addition to the repeal of the duties on raw sugar, there is also a lessening of the rates on the refined sugar. Sugars above 14 D.S. and all refined sugars are taxed 8-10c. per pound;¶ on molasses the duty was fixed at 1½ cents per gallon. The Act passed** later on

*15th October, 1890.

†From the standpoint of revenue they had been of little value. During 1868-93, the average yearly revenue from this source was only $20,839.00. *Vide* Table I. in appendix.

‡" Kiln dried, and ground into meal for human food."

§54-55 Vict., Cap. 44.

||*Vide* Table III. in appendix.

¶Under the Act of 1886 these had been charged ½c. and 30 per cent.

**54-5 Vict., Cap. 31.

in the session, providing for the payment of a bounty of $1 per hundred weight on beet-root sugar " produced in Canada wholly from beets produced therein " is to be taken as a complementary part of the Tariff legislation of the year ; it serves to attract attention to the fact that the protective phase was by no means lost sight of amid the various amendments.

As a consequence of the remission of duties upon sugar, revenue had to be raised from other sources. The Government made use of the method which plays such an important part in modern financing, and imposed heavier duties on tobacco and spirits. Viewed from the standpoint of expediency, and leaving out of consideration all questions of ethics, such taxes are excellent because the Government is sure of a fairly steady revenue from them. On malt the duty was placed at 2 cents per pound*, or about 3 cents per gallon on beer ; from this source there was expected a revenue of $500,000 ; an excise duty of 20 cents per gallon was imposed on distilled spirits—this was expected to increase the revenue by about $600,000 ; on tobacco an increase in duty of 6 cents per pound was expected to give an increase in revenue of about $400,000. Thus the total increase in revenue expected from these sources was $1,500,000 ; the total gross reduction in revenue was $3,500,000—leaving a net reduction in customs rates of $2,000,000. The average specific duty on spirituous liquors now stood at $2.12½ per gallon—an increase of 12½ cents per gallon. It will be seen that these increases affected, partly the excise, partly the customs.†

There was no general Tariff amendment in 1892. The duties which had, since 1886, been imposed on fish and fish products imported into Canada from Newfoundland were now remitted.‡ The customs rates were made to press more heavily on tobacco and molasses, and more protection was extended to the manufacture of fine leather§ by the inclusion in the free list of several articles used in the manufacture. The duty imposed on eggs was retaliatory. The drafters of the McKinley Tariff had imposed a duty upon eggs. This was met, on the part of the Canadian Government, by the imposition of a tax of 5 cents per dozen on eggs ; this would, on the average amount to 33⅓ per cent.

On tobaccos the chief changes were as follows :

— —	Rate of 1892.	Rate of 1891.
Cut tobacco	55 cents and 15 per cent	40 cents and 12½ per cent.
Manufactured tobacco and snuff	45 cents and 15 per cent	35 cents and 12½ per cent.

The two elements present in the provisions with reference to the sugar industry, are retaliatory duties and paternalistic protection. It is provided that in case a country which exports sugar to Canada, discriminates against Canada that the Governor-General-in-Council may suspend the ordinary regulations and apply the following rates on :

Sugar below 14 D.S. 1 cent per pound and for every { This would vary from 25 additional degree or fraction thereof 3½c. per cwt. { per cent. to 33⅓ per cent.

*This made the malt and beer duty in Canada 7 cents, as compared with 4 cents in Great Britain, and 3⁷⁄₁₀ cents in the United States. The malt duty was in 1891 decreased to 1½ cents per pound ; prior to 1891 it had stood at 1c. per pound.

†In addition to these changes a duty of 5 cents per hundred weight was imposed on coarse salt.

‡By Order-in-Council of May 27th, 1892.

§This manufacture had already been protected : now the form of protection was somewhat changed and degras and oleostearine, which are used in the process of manufacture, were placed on the free list.

Sugar above 14 D.S., 2c. per pound. { This would vary from 34.75 per cent. to 47.05 per cent.

Molasses, 25 per cent............ { This would vary from 10c. to 12½c. per gallon, according to quality.

There is a suggestion of paternalism in the prohibitory provision with reference to the lower grades of molasses. The Government stated its intention of imposing a prohibitory duty on molasses which did not show more than 20° or 30° of saccharine material. It was held that such inferior grades of molasses were unfit for use. Accordingly the following subdivision was made with reference to the duties. The original rate for all molasses had been 1½ cents per gallon; under the new arrangement molasses between 40° and 50° were still taxed at the old rate, while, on molasses under 40°, the old rate was still imposed plus 1 cent per gallon for each degree or fraction of a degree less than 40° and besides this 2½ cents per gallon when not imported direct.

In 1890* in order to extend protection to the home industry, a duty of 25 per cent. had been imposed on all grades of binding twine. This tax pressed heavily on the farming classes and raised much popular discontent : accordingly in 1893 the Act was amended and a reduction made in the rate of duty. The finished article was now taxed at 12½ per cent., while the unfinished, when imported to be further manufactured, was taxed at 10 per cent.† The only other change made in this year was the extension of the period during which mining machinery of a kind not manufactured in Canada could be imported free of duty.‡

Prior to the amendment of the Tariff, in 1894, an attempt was made to ascertain what changes were desired by the people ; with this end in view, the representatives of the leading industries throughout the country were interviewed by the Comptrollers of Customs and Inland Revenue and other members of the administration.§ The information so obtained was used as data for the revision. In this revision there are to be found many of the general tendencies of reform which have appeared throughout this period. The Budget Speech introducing the amended Tariff shows that the Finance Minister‖ was much more ready than some of his predecessors, to present a reason for his Tariff policy. Although the belief in protection is evident yet there appears the significant statement, " If there is to be a protective system at all, everybody knows that it must be higher in its inception than as the years gradually pass, when industries have become established and when the industrial development of the country grows apace."** The facts of history would hardly justify the conclusion that, in the earlier days of the National Policy, those entrusted with the management of the Tariff, were well aware of the limitations to be placed upon a Protective Policy or were possessed of systematic views on the process through which, as time went on, a Protective Policy should pass. The application of protection to the various industries hardly pretended to proceed on any scientific principle ; considerations of the present rather than the ultimate gain exercised most influence.

*53 Vict., Cap. 20, Sec. 10, item 184.
†56 Vict., Cap. 16. Sec. 10, item 184.
‡By the Act of 1890 (53 Vict., Cap. 20, Sec. 11, item 291) provision had been made for the importation of such machinery free of duty during a period of three years. By the Act of this year this term is extended until July 16th, 1896.
§Such a peripatetic system of investigation, on the face of it at least, would seem better fitted to the end in view than that adopted at Washington in the late Tariff revision. There, when the Wilson Bill was being drafted, representatives of the various industries were summoned to appear before the Ways and Means Committee at Washington. It may reasonably be claimed that the system of investigation adopted in Canada gave more opportunity for the claims of the smaller industries being heard.
‖Hon. G. E. Foster.
**Budget Speech.

The statement of the Finance Minister illustrates his own views of the process of tariff evolution, under a protective system.

It was stated in the Budget Speech, that "one main attempt had been to simplify and make clear the Tariff" * and also that "the time for revision has come . . the time for a complete examination of the whole matter of our Tariff arrangements in order that the anomalies existing might be done away with and that the Tariff might be brought down to the existing circumstances and changed conditions not only in Canada but in foreign countries at the present time."† This should furnish an excellent text for Tariff Reform. In the practical application of this, especially in the amendments, there may, however, be found some limitations. One other statement substantiates what has been said, in an earlier part of this essay, namely that during the earlier period of the enforcement of the National Policy the needs of the producer were closely looked to, but that during this later period more attention was paid to the consumer. This is shown in the following: "‡The prime object in view has been to cheapen the cost of manufactures in this country, to cheapen the cost at which the goods issue from the factory itself." It is characteristic of the earlier stages of a protectionist movement that most attention is paid to the manufacturer, in fact it is of the essence of the movement that the consumer should be willing to put up with a temporary inconvenience, in order that the home manufacture should be built up. When the needs of the consumer appear to the Minister, under a régime of protection, to demand attention it is sufficient evidence, that to him, at least, the day of high protection is passing and that the manufactures of the country are becoming able to stand alone.

Both the Canadian and the American Tariff revisions of this year suffered considerable change in their progress through the legislative chambers. The Wilson Bill, as at first drafted, although it retained protective features, was yet a movement towards Tariff Reform. When it left the House of Representatives it practically expressed the will of the administration on the subject. In the process of the Bill through the Senate many changes were made, and although on the whole the pressure of customs taxation was lightened, yet the distinctive characteristic of Tariff Reform was not so markedly present as in the original draft. The Canadian Tariff, as presented to the House in draft form, represented the views of the Finance Department with reference to the advisability of Tariff Reform. During the progress of the Bill through the committee stage many amendments were made; delegations from interests affected made their wishes known, and the result was that the Tariff, as finally enacted, although lessening somewhat the average pressure of duty, differed in many particulars from the original draft. For the purposes of study it will be found convenient to consider first the proposed Tariff; then the amendments will demand consideration, in that they show the changes which had to be made in order to pacify the conflicting and divergent interests which are so numerous and clamorous under a protective system.

It was calculated that, as a consequence of the change in the Tariff, the uniform pressure of taxation over all would be 28 per cent.—a reduction of 2 per cent. as compared with the average rate of 1893. It was estimated that this reduction would throw off from $1,500,000 to $1,600,000. The accuracy of these calculations cannot be verified until the trade returns for the year are available.

---

*Budget Speech.   †Ibid.   ‡Ibid.

In the Tariff two main tendencies are manifested, one towards simplication of enumeration, the other towards the substitution of *ad valorem* for specific and compound duties. The following may be taken as an example of both tendencies. Under the old rate cotton batts had been subdivided as follows :

Cotton batts, undyed .... 2 cents and 15 per cent.
do   dyed 3   "   15   "

Under the new rate both are included under an *ad valorem* duty of 22½ per cent. This tendency towards the substitution of *ad valorem* duties for those hitherto in force, is most noticeable in cottons. There are some twenty-seven dutiable articles of cotton specified under the heading of textiles. Under the old list fifteen of these were subject to a compound duty; under the new list only three. In all there are in this Tariff some thirty changes from specific or compound duties to *ad valorem*.

Something has been said with reference to the tendencies apparent in the Tariff, as also with reference to the estimated pressure of customs duties over all. This will indicate the general tendency. For purposes of more detailed investigation it will serve if a fairly representative list is chosen and a comparison instituted between the rates of 1894 and those of former years. The following articles will be taken for this purpose : Spirits, tobacco, agricultural implements, agricultural produce, cotton, wool, iron and steel, sugar, leather and chemicals.

Spirits. The rate remains unchanged.

Tobaccos. The duties are unchanged.

Agricultural products. Here the changes were only in a few of the articles. This was in keeping with the general plan, for it was stated that "it is not the policy of the Government to decrease in any material degree the protection at present afforded to the agricultural interests of the country." The following table gives the chief changes :

	New rate.	Old rate.	Average change.
Live hogs	25 per cent.	2 cents per lb.....	5 to 8 per ct. reduction.
Salt meats.................	20 "	3 "	10 to 17½ "
Lard	25 "	2 "	5 per cent. "
Tallow	20 "	1 "	Slight increase.
Apples, beans, buckwheat, peas, potatoes and rye† ..	Unchanged........	Unchanged.	
Barley and Indian corn‡....	"	"	
Oatmeal........	50 cts. per bbl.§	½ cent per lb‖..........	10.11 per ct. reduction.
Live animals	20 per cent	25 per cent	5 per ct. reduction.
Tomatoes	20 cts. and 10 per cent ..	30 cts and 10 per cent...	10 cts. "
Blackberries, gooseberries, raspberries, etc	2 cts. (about 38.71 per ct.)	3 cts. (about 58.06 per ct.)	19.35 per cent. reduction.

Agricultural implements. A reduction of 15 per cent. was made in the rate ; a duty of 20 per cent. being substituted for the former rate of 35 per cent. The duty on smaller implements for farm use, *e.g.* scythes, hayknives, forks, rakes and hoes, remained at 35 per cent.

*Budget speech.
†There is a provision for a statutory offer of reciprocity.
‡There is a statutory offer of reciprocity. In the case of Indian corn there is a drawback of 90 per ct.
§About 10.52 per cent. The average percentage charge is calculated on the basis of a wholesale trade list.
‖About 20.63 per cent.

Cotton. As has been mentioned, changes from compound to *ad valorem* duties took place in this list. The following table contains the articles upon which a compound duty is replaced by another rate of duty :

—	Old rate.	New rate.
Cotton batting (not bleached, etc.).............	2 cents and 15 per cent.....	22½ per cent.
" " (bleached, etc.)	3 " 15 "	22½ "
" batts (unbleached, etc.)	2 " 15 "	22½ "
" " (bleached, etc.)	3 " 15 "	22½ "
" wadding (unbleached, etc.)......	2 " 15 "	22½ "
" " (bleached, etc.)	3 " 15 "	22½ "
" yarn	2 " 15 "	25 "
" "	3 " 15 "	25 "
" grey (unbleached)	1 ct. per sq. yd. and 15 per ct	25 "
" bleached	" "	30 "
" collars	24 cts. per doz. and 30 per ct.	24 cts and 25 per cent.
" cuffs	4 " " "	4 " "
" shirts..............................	$1 " · "	30 per cent. when under $3.00 per doz. When over $3.00 per doz., $1.00 per doz and 25 per cent.
" webbing (non elastic)	2 cts. and 15 per cent	25 per cent.
" cordage	1¼ " 10 ."	"

There are twelve articles on which *ad valorem* rates are charged both in the old Tariff and the new. The average charge on these under the old list was 26.66 per cent. Now the average rate is 25.67 per cent., or a net average reduction of 1 per cent. The reduction is, however, really greater than appears ; on one of the articles* the duty had, for purposes of revenue, been increased 10 per cent., and the increase goes for to counterbalance the decrease on the other articles.

Woolens. In woolens the chief change is in the sub stitutionof *ad valorem* for compound duties. The following table illustrates this substitution :

—	Old rate.	New rate.
Woolen yarn	10 cents and 20 per cent	27½ per cent.
Wool cloth..........	10 " "	30 "
Dress goods	10 " "	22½ "
Knitted goods	10 " "	35 "
Carpets	10 " " ...	35 "
Clothing	10 " " ...	32½ "

This change means at the same time, on the whole, a reduction in duty. Take for example woolen yarn ;· taking the average value as $1 per pound, this change would mean a reduction of 2½ per cent. The more equitable pressure has also to be remembered. The change in woolens is especially noticeable as the compound duties had been much in favor on this item.

Iron and Steel. In the Tariff list of 1894 there are some sixty items under this heading. This does not mean, however, that only sixty articles of iron and

---

*The article in question is velvet and velveteens. The duty was now placed at 20 per cent.

steel are dealt with, for most of the items include several varieties of iron and steel manufactured products. There is on the whole a tendency towards general reduction of duties. There is not present the same general tendency to favor *ad valorem* duties as is shown in other sections. One provision that is present in the old Act, in several instances, is also present here, namely, a provision that the specific duty imposed shall be equivalent to at least a certain percentage. For example, if a specific duty of $10 per ton is imposed on an article, then there is occasionally a proviso that this shall be equal to at least 30 per cent. or 35 per cent.,* as the case may. The estimated reduction of duties on metals and manufactures was about $350,000.

It has been contended, by those who advocate a high Tariff on iron, that the cardinal weakness of the iron schedule of 1887 was the fact that the rate of duty on scrap iron was very much lower than that on puddled bar, blooms and billets with which it came into competition.† From the standpoint of protection this low rate of duty on scrap iron was certainly a weakness in the protective policy and went far to nullify the protective intent. In the manufacture of bar iron, either puddled bar or scrap iron may be used. The puddled bar is the product of pig iron. It was the intention of the Government, when imposing the duties of 1887, to cause more puddled bar to be used in the manufacture of bar iron and, as a necessary consequence of this, to cause a greater manufacture of pig iron. The duty on puddled bar was fixed at $13 per ton with the intention of securing the market to the home product. Owing to the low rate of duty imposed on scrap iron, those engaged in the manufacture of bar iron found it more to their advantage to import scrap. As a consequence of this practically no bar iron was manufactured from puddled bars, and so the Government policy, instead of ensuring the development of the higher branches of the iron trade, had a directly opposite effect. This state of affairs had continued from 1887 to 1894. A change was now made. The $2 duty already imposed was forthwith increased to $3, and it was provided that after January 1st, 1895, it should be raised to $4. The intention in so doing was to make the Tariff on iron completely protective. The duty was intended to be practically prohibitory.‡ While the duty on scrap iron was increased, the duty on puddled bar was decreased from $9 to $5. This reduction was justified on the ground that it would reduce the cost of merchantable iron to the country. The provision already existing for a bounty of $2 per ton on pig iron was retained,§ and a similar provision was enacted in the case of puddled bar and steel billets. In addition it was provided that these bounties should run for five years from the date of the enactment.‖

---

*The favorite rate under such conditions is 35 per cent. The evident intention is to combine in its operation the advantages of both specific and *ad valorem* duties. If the specific charge fell below the required percentage, it would have to be adapted to the altered conditions. The development of industry and the gradual cheapening of industrial processes, ensure that, on the average, the specific charge will be more than the proportion required.

†*Vide The Iron Industry*, p. 24. This is a pamphlet which was read before the Mining Association of Quebec, by Mr. G. E. Drummond, Vice-president of the Association.

‡"Under that duty it is supposed that not a very great deal of foreign scrap will be imported. Our object is to induce the manufacture of bar iron from the iron of the country—from puddled bars." Budget Speech, reply of Hon. Mr. Foster to question of Sir Richard Cartwright.

§During the fiscal year 1893-4 this bounty was paid on 48,000 tons.

‖This was moved on July 18th, 1894. It is to hold until March 26th, 1894. In the case of foundries started after the present but before the ultimate date, the bounty is to hold for five years from time of starting.

The general rate on iron goods not especially provided for is reduced to 27½ per cent., a reduction of 2½ per cent. as compared with the rate of 1887. The following table gives the changes of importance.

—	Budget rate of 1894.	Rate of 1887.
Scrap iron	$4 per ton	$2 per ton.
Slabs, blooms, etc	85 "	$9 "
Bars	$10 "	$13 "
Plough-plates, etc	5 per cent	12½ per cent.
Railway rails	30 "	$6 per ton.
Railway fish plates	30 "	$12 "
Band and hoop iron	5 "	$13 "
Stoves and castings	27½ "	$16 " but not less than 30 per cent.
Iron bridges, etc	30 "	1½c. per lb., " 35 "
Locomotives	35 "	30 per cent.
Drawn boiler tubing	7½ "	15 "
Builders' hardware	32½ "	35 "
Bolts, washers, etc	½c. and 20 per cent.	½c. and 30 per cent.
Tacks, etc	1c. per 1,000.	2c. per 1,000.
Horseshoe and horseshoe nails	30 per cent.	1½c. per lb., but not less than 35 per cent.
Iron wire nails	¾c. per lb.	1½c. " " 35 "
Scales and balances	30 per cent.	35 per cent.
Adzes, hatchets, etc	30 "	35 "

A comparison of the iron goods chargeable with *ad valorem* rates under both Acts gives the following result :

Average duties on goods chargeable with *ad valorem*
  duties in old list............................ 30.45 per cent.
Average duties on same goods chargeable with *ad*
  valorem duties in new list .... 21.74   "

Cross tendencies are shown in the goods subject to compound duties. For example, on wrought iron tubing and pipes the specific component of the compound duty is increased 4-10c.; on wrought iron or steel rivets the *ad valorem* element is decreased 5 per cent.; on skates the specific component is reduced by 10c. This illustrates the somewhat erratic nature of the changes in the compound duties. On the whole there is a reduction.

The action of the free list must, as usual, be taken as complementary to the operation of the dutiable list. The addition to the free list is by way of concession to the dairying interests.*

Sugars. In sugars the changes are few, and may at once be indicated by a short table.

—	New rate.	Old rate.
Molasses	Unchanged	
Sugar candy and confectionery	35 per cent.	1½c. and 35 per.
Sugar above No. 16 D.S.† (refined, etc.)	1½c.	8-10c.

* Steel cream separators are added to the free list.

† The raising of the standard from No. 14 D.S. to No. 16 D.S. admitted free sugar, fitted for culinary and table purposes.

Chemicals. In the case of acetic acid and pyroligneous acid for dyers, the duty is changed from 1c. and 20 per cent. to 25 per cent. On the whole there is a decrease both in the specific and *ad valorem* rates.

Leather. On leather board and leatheroid an *ad valorem* rate of 20 per cent. is substituted for the former specific charge of 3c. per pound. On eight other items, which bear an *ad valorem* duty, under both the old Act and the new, the average new duty is 17.825 per cent. as compared with the former average rate of 20.625 per cent.

In the discussion of the pressure of duties upon agricultural produce the reciprocity clause has already been referred to. This clause differs in great degree from the reciprocity provisions of earlier years, in that it is not so comprehensive. It has to do with agricultural products, but it does not contain a comprehensive list of these. The imports into Canada of the various articles provided for under the reciprocity clause warrant the conclusion that the provision is more semblance than reality. These imports in 1892* amounted to less than $200,000, or to be more exact, to $161,621. The most important items are apples, of which $80,367 were imported, and potatoes, of which there was an import of $48,287.†

The most important changes in the free list are with reference to acids, chemicals and lumber. The policy pursued by the Government in placing acids on the free list may best be indicated by quoting the words of the Finance. Minister: "Generally, I may say that all acids, drugs, dye-stuffs, everything which is necessary for tanning, in the manufacturing processes and the like, have been taken from the dutiable list and placed on the free list."‡ The Government investigations, prior to the amendment of the Tariff, showed that the lumber combines exercised considerable pressure on the people, especially in the Northwest. There the rougher grades of lumber were in much demand for use in the construction of farm dwellings, and the settlers were practically at the mercy of the combine. To redress this grievance lumber was placed on the free list. Sundry changes, in this direction, had, from time to time, been made; but the amendment of this year was more comprehensive in that squared lumber, shingles and, in general, the rougher grades of timber used in house-building were placed on the free list. The average rate of charge on these had been about 20 per cent. Although this change was made, it is to be borne in mind that the Tariff Act reposed in the hands of the Governor-General-in-Council power to impose export duties on the articles included in the lumber schedule in case any duties were imposed on them by foreign countries.§

The amendments to the Tariff in its way through committee were numerous.‖ In so far as there is any appreciable principle shown it is totake specific duties into favor once more. On the whole there is a tendency towards an increased rate of duty, *i.e.*, as compared with the budget rates.

* *Vide* Statistical Year Book for 1892, p. 248.

† The articles which, in terms of the statutory provision, are admitted free of duty on reciprocal terms are apples, beans, buckwheat, peas, potatoes, rye, hay, vegetables and barley, and, as has already been indicated, the imports of these commodities were of minor importance. In another section of the Tariff provision is made for the importation of corn, free of duty, on reciprocal terms. In 1892 the imports of corn amounted to $862,455, while the exports only amounted to $222. (pp. 348-9 Statistical Year Book for 1892.)

‡ *Vide* Budget Speech.

§ The provision is as follows: "Provided that if any country shall impose a duty upon the articles in the schedule enumerated, or any of these, when imported into such country from Canada it shall be lawful for the Governor-General-in-Council, from time to time by proclamation published in *The Canada Gazette*, to declare that the following export duties, or any of them shall be chargeable upon logs exported into such country from Canada, viz., pine, Douglas fir, spruce, fir, balsam, cedar and hemlock logs, not exceeding three dollars per thousand feet, board measure."

‖ There were one hundred and twenty changes.

In the iron list various changes, which do not proceed on any well-defined system, are made. In some instances the *ad valorem* rate is increased; in others a specific rate is substituted for it, and in others a *quasi ad valorem* duty is imposed.* On the whole the tendency is to impose a duty which, while heavier than the Budget rate, is still lower than that in force in 1892-3. The various changes and cross tendencies, as well as the relative favor shown to various forms of duties, may be seen from the following table, which contains the changes of importance.

—	Budget rate.	Tariff as enacted.
Railway fish-plates	30 per cent	$10 per ton.
Band and hoop	5 "	$10 "
Car wheels and axles..........	35 "	$20 " but not less than 35 per cent.
Rolled, beams, channels, etc	12½ "	35 per cent., but not less than $10 per ton.
Iron and steel forgings..........	35 "	35 " ' " $15 "
Tinned and enamelled wares	30 "	35 "
Bolts, washers, etc..............	1c. per lb., and 20 per cent.	1c. per lb., and 25 per cent.
Iron wire nails	¾c. per lb....	1c. per lb.
Nuts, etc	1c. per lb., and 20 per cent.	1c. per lb., and 25 per cent. ; not to be less than 30 per cent.
Adzes, hatchets, etc	30 per cent	35 per cent.
Shovels and spades.............	35 "	50c. per dozen, and 25 per cent.
Tacks, etc....................	1c. per lb.	1½c. per lb.

The rate on oatmeal had been changed; a specific charge of 50 cents per barrel having been substituted for the former charge of ½ cent. per pound. An *ad valorem* duty of 20 per cent. is now imposed, which almost wholly neutralizes the former reduction. Taking the value of a barrel of oatmeal as $4.75, then the old rate of ½ cent per pound on 196 pounds would give an average duty of 20.63 per cent. ; the Budget rate of 50 cents per barrel would give a duty of 10.52 per cent. while the new duty is 20 per cent. Thus, as contrasted with the Budget rate,' there is an increase of 9.48 per cent., while as contrasted with the rate of 1893 there is an' infinitesimal reduction of .63 per cent.

In the duties on woolens the old rates had been wholly compound; when the Tariff changes were first formulated these compound duties were for the most part replaced by *ad valorem* rates. Now there is another change, and in five instances *ad valorem* rates are replaced by compound. When these compound rates are contrasted with the compound rates in existence in 1893, it is seen, however, that there is somewhat of a change. The specific component of the compound duty is lessened, while at the same time the *ad valorem* element is increased. On five items, on which the *ad valorem* duties of the budget give way to the compound duties of the Bill, there is an average rate of 5 3-5c. and 28 per cent., as contrasted with the former average compound duty of 9c. and 21 per cent. In one case the *ad valorem* rate is reduced by 7½ per cent.†

A few other changes may be indicated. Cleaned rice is restored to the old rate of 1¼c. per pound; the budget rate was 1c. On uncleaned rice the rate is lowered by ¼ of a cent. Photographers' supplies received an increased protection

---

* *E.g.*, the duty of 35 per cent. imposed, by the budget, on iron and steel forgings is replaced by a *quasi ad valorem* duty of "35 per cent., but not less than $15 per ton."

† The Budget rate on yarns was 27½ per cent. ; they are now listed at 20 per cent.

of 5 per cent. The rate had already been raised to 30 per cent. by the Budget. In the case of the finer grades of leather the rate is increased by 2½ per cent. The duty on coal oil is reduced 1 1-5c. per gallon.

A few changes were made in the free list. Salt and eggs had been rendered free of duty ; they were now once more placed on the dutiable list. The old rate of 5c. per dozen was reimposed on eggs ; while on salt there was imposed a duty of 5 cents per hundred weight when in bulk, and 7½c. per hundred weight when in packages. The old duty of 20 per cent. was reimposed on shingles. In pursuance of the policy outlined in the Budget speech, there was a further inclusion in the free list of articles ancillary to the dyeing industry.

The year 1894 witnessed Tariff amendment in the United States as well as in Canada. The Tariff legislation of the United States, has undoubtedly, from time to time, exerted an important influence upon the Tariff of Canada.* This fact, coupled with the somewhat similar course of amendment which befell both Bills in committee, would render a comparative study of these two Tariffs one of especial interest. Without attempting any so ambitious general discussion, it will, perhaps, suffice to give a tabular summary, indicating the pressure of duties on some of the leading commodities of both countries, and thereby suggest the resemblances and differences in the two Tariffs.

—	United States Tariff.	Canadian Tariff.
Poultry	2c. per lb	20 per cent.
Beef	20 per cent	3c. per lb.
Mutton	20 "	35 per cent.
Pork	20 "	25 "
Butter	4c. per lb	4c. per lb.
Honey	1½c. "	3c. "
Smoked fish	¾c. "	1c. "
Barley	30 per cent	30 per cent.
Hay	$2 per ton	$2 per ton.
Hops	8c. per lb	6c. per lb.
Onions	20c. per bush	25 per cent.
Peas	20c. "	10c. per bush.
Potatoes	15c. "	15c. "
Apples	20 per cent	40c. per bbl.
Plums	1½c. per lb	25 per cent.
Horses	20 "	20 "
Cattle	20 "	20 "
Wool (raw)	Free	Free.
Lumber	"	"
Eggs	3c. per dozen	5c. per dozen.

Canada has gone through various stages of Tariff policy, from low revenue tariff to comparatively high protection, and for all the differing Tariffs there is found a relative justification in the conditions of the time. The National Policy was originally intended to develop Canadian industries, obtain reciprocity with the United States, and relieve Canada from the effects of financial depression. The reciprocity idea, however, was only the "ruse of war " of shrewd politicians. The building up of the national industries, and the consequent increase in revenue to be obtained from the heightened import duties were what those in power laid most stress upon. For the time the consumer was willing to put up with the

* Some discussion of this will be found in the note in the appendix " The influence of the Tariff legislation of the United States upon the Canadian Tariff."

enhanced cost in order to build up home manufactures. As time went on he found the pressure more and more irksome, and the Tariff amendment of 1894 represents in some degree an attempt to meet the needs of the consumers. Despite the fact that amendments have from, time to time, taken place, the average rate of duty in the later periods of the operation of the National Policy is much higher* than in the earlier years. But in qualification of this it must be remembered that the various forms of taxable commodity have been more thoroughly sought out than formerly, and that though arbitrary pressure is probably inseparable from a protective system, yet the pressure is not quite so arbitrary as it once was.

The popular desire for Tariff Reform makes the amendment of 1894 especially interesting. In earlier years the Finance Ministers were, to a great extent, under the control of the protected interests. Nowadays the Finance Department shows more *desire* to adjust the Tariff so as to meet the needs of all classes ; but the events of the committee stage of the Tariff Amendment Act of 1894 show that the Finance Department has not yet obtained freedom, to do as it deems best, in matters pertaining to the Tariff.

It is an economic commonplace that, when once a protective policy is adopted, in a country possessed of representative institutions, it is exceedingly difficult for the Government, on account of the pressure brought to bear upon it by the protected interests, to readjust the Tariff. In Canada the protective policy in vogue co-operates with the peculiar position of the country to render Tariff reform an exceedingly gradual matter. The greater part of the revenue of the Dominion is obtained from the customs duties ;† and the increasing demands for Government expenditure cause the administration to look with favor—from the financial standpoint, if from no other—upon the continuance of the present system, which insures a comparatively stable revenue. When this dependence upon the customs duties is coupled with the clamorous influence brought to bear by the protected classes, the task of the Government when undertaking a revision of the Tariff is a difficult one ; and the revision itself must of necessity proceed very gradually. Reasoning from the conditions of the past to the probabilities of the future it may safely be concluded that Tariff Reform in Canada will be achieved, not by a sudden reduction, but only by very gradual steps.

---

* See Table I. in Appendix.

† During the years 1868-93, 74 per cent. of the whole amount of taxation was derived from customs duties. In the United Kingdom in the same year the proportion of customs duties to total revenue was 26 per cent., while in the United States it was 55 per cent. The *per capita* payment of customs duties in 1893 was $4.22 in Canada, $2.50 in the United Kingdom, and $3.05 in the United States. (Statistical Year Book, 1893, p. 712.)

APPENDIX.

CANADIAN STATUTES DEALING WITH THE CUSTOMS 1867-94.

1867—31 Vict., cap. 6 ; 31 Vict., cap. 7.
1868 —31 Vict.,cap.43; 31 Vict.,cap. 44.
1869—No Act.
1870—33 Vict., cap. 9.
1871—34 Vict., cap. 10.
1872—35 Vict., cap. 11 ; 35 Vict., cap. 12 ; 35 Vict., cap. 37.
1873—36 Vict., cap. 39.
1874—37 Vict., cap. 6.
1875—38 Vict., cap. 35.
1876—No Act.
1877—40 Vict.,cap.10; 40 Vict.,cap.11.
1878—No Act.
1879—42 Vict., cap. 15.
1880—43 Vict., cap. 18.
1881—44 Vict., cap. 10.
1882—45 Vict., cap. 6.

1883—46 Vict.,cap.12; 46 Vict.,cap. 13.
1884—47 Vict.,cap.29; 47 Vict.,cap.30.
1885—48 Vict., cap. 61.
1886—49 Vict., cap. 32 ; 49 Vict., cap. 37 ; 49 Vict., cap. 38.
1887—50-1 Vict., cap. 39.
1888—51 Vict., cap. 14; 51 Vict., cap. 15.
1889—52 Vict., cap. 14.
1890—53 Vict., cap. 20 ; 53 Vict., cap. 21.
1891—54-5 Vict., cap. 44 ; 54-5 Vict., cap. 45 ; 54-5 Vict., cap. 31.
1892—55-6 Vict., cap. 21.
1893—56 Vict., cap. 16.
1894—57-8 Vict., cap. 3.

TABLE I.—Table of duties collected, and percentages of duty, on the average, on dutiable goods.

Years ending June 30th.	Total exports.	Total imports.	Imports for home consumption.	Duty.	Free goods.	Percentage of duty on goods entered for home consumption.	Export duties,
	$ c.	$ c.	$ c.	$ c.	$ c.	per cent.	$ c.
1868	57,507,888 00	73,459,644 00	71,985,306 00	8,819,431 63	28,329,610 00	20.22	17,986 00
1869	60,474,781 00	76,415,165 00	67,402,170 00	8,298,909 71	26,232,928 00	20.18	14,102 00
1870	73,573,490 00	74,814,339 00	71,237,603 00	9,462,940 44	26,110,181 00	20.95	37,912 00
1871	74,173,618 00	91,093,971 00	86,947,482 00	11,843,655 75	26,853,130 00	19.70	36,066 00
1872	82,639,663 00	111,430,527 00	107,709,116 00	13,045,493 50	39,163,398 00	19.03	24,809 00
1873	89,789,922 00	128,011,281 00	127,514,594 00	13,017,730 17	56,105,398 00	17.11	20,152 00
1874	89,351,928 00	128,213,582 00	127,404,109 00	14,421,852 67	51,168,316 00	19.32	14,565 00
1875	77,886,979 00	123,010,283 00	119,618,657 00	15,361,382 12	41,477,229 00	19.53	7,243 00
1876	80,966,435 00	93,210,346 00	94,733,218 00	12,833,114 48	34,489,872 00	21.30	4,500 00
1877	75,875,393 00	99,327,962 00	96,300,483 00	12,548,451 09	35,380,523 00	20.63	4,103 00
1878	79,323,667 00	93,081,787 00	91,199,577 00	12,795,693 17	31,422,988 00	21.50	4,161 00
1879	71,491,255 00	81,964,427 00	80,341,408 00	12,937,540 06	24,911,596 00	23.35	4,272 00
1880	87,911,458 00	86,489,747 00	71,872,349 00	14,138,849 22	17,593,382 00	26.11	8,896 00
1881	98,290,823 00	105,330,840 00	91,611,604 00	18,500,285 97	19,990,879 00	24.56	8,140 00
1882	102,137,203 00	119,419,500 00	112,648,927 00	21,708,837 43	26,891,494 00	26.40	8,810 00
1883	98,085,804 00	132,254,022 00	123,137,019 00	23,172,308 97	31,548,680 00	25.32	9,755 00
1884	91,406,496 00	116,397,043 00	108,180,644 00	20,164,963 37	28,170,146 00	25.30	8,516 00
1885	89,238,361 00	108,941,486 00	102,710,019 00	19,133,558 99	29,440,401 00	26.11	12,305 00
1886	85,251,314 00	104,424,561 00	99,602,691 00	19,448,123 70	28,943,875 00	27.52	20,726 00
1887	89,515,811 00	112,892,236 00	105,639,428 00	23,479,705 83	27,518,747 00	30.00	31,397 00
1888	90,203,000 00	110,894,630 00	102,847,100 00	22,209,691 53	31,625,804 00	31.04	21,772 00
1889	89,189,167 00	115,224,931 00	109,673,047 00	23,784,523 23	34,623,057 00	30.34	42,207 00
1890	96,749,149 00	121,858,241 00	112,765,584 00	24,014,908 07	35,659,298 00	31.93	93,674 00
1891	98,417,296 00	119,967,628 00	113,345,124 00	23,481,069 13	38,809,088 00	31.49	64,803 00
1892	113,963,375 00	127,486,068 00	116,978,943 00	20,650,581 53	47,818,206 00	29.75	108 00
1893	118,564,352 00	129,074,268 00	121,705,030 00	21,154,171 00	51,831,459 00	30.28	

TABLE II.—Percentage of duty on total imports—dutiable and free.

Year.	Per cent.	Year.	Per cent.	Year.	Per cent.
1868	12.00	1877	12.63	1886	18.60
1869	11.78	1878	13.74	1887	19.87
1870	12.05	1879	15.78	1888	20.03
1871	12.32	1880	16.34	1889	20 60
1872	11.70	1881	17.56	1890	19.63
1873	10.17	1882	18.18	1891	19.52
1874	11.25	1883	17.52	1892	16.13
1875	12.48	1884	17.32	1893	17.38
1876	13.76	1885	17.55		

TABLE III.—Sugar entered for home consumption in Canada, 1879-90, and duty thereon.

Year.	Quantity.	Value.	Duty.	Rate per cent.
	Pounds.	$ c.	$ c.	
1879	109,463,915 00	6,186,226 00	2,595,074 00	41.95
1880	116,847.050 00	3,904,287 00	2,026,692 00	51.93
1881	136,406,513 00	5,110,993 00	2,459,142 00	48.00
1882	135,329,697 00	4,846,066 00	2,999,761 00	47.50
1883	152,729,569 00	5,091,530 00	2,467,730 00	48.00
1884	173,742,477 00	5,509,429 00	2,609,509 00	47.36
1885	200,011,541 00	5,100,478 00	2,544,920 00	50.00
1886	177,397,735 00	4,573,574 00	2,303,397 00	50.30
1887	200,466,072 00	4,862,042 00	3,167,528 00	65.20
1888	201,839,821 00	5,154,143 00	3,433,334 00	61.50
1889	223,841,171 00	5,837,895 00	3,675,724 00	62.96
1890	174,075,720 00	5,186,158 00	2,851,547 00	55.20

TABLE IV.—Imports of iron and steel into Canada for home consumption 1868-87.

Year.	$ c.	Year.	$ c.
1868	6,885,365 00	1878	9,398,306 00
1869	7,385,780 00	1879	7,962,295 00
1870	7,750,867 00	1880	10,128,660 00
1871	10,808,645 00	1881	12,955,855 00
1872	15,913,179 00	1882	17,499,488 00
1873	25,435,620 00	1883	20,080,274 00
1874	20,700,387 00	1884	14,790,727 00
1875	18,199,193 00	1885	11,415,713 00
1876	12,965,117 00	1886	11,053,365 00
1877	11,082,321 00	1887	13,595,046 00

NOTE ON "PROTECTION *VERSUS* FREE TRADE."*†

Protection has appealed much to the national sentiment—a fact which is illustrated in the popular name of the Canadian protective policy. Free trade, on the other hand, is more cosmopolitan in tone. The free trade advocate believes in a process of evolution which will ensure the survival of "the fittest;" the protectionist, on the other hand, wishes to give the home industry an advantage at least for the time being—and he may look forward to a time when the differential advantage afforded by a protective duty will be removed.

Free trade advocates have at times made their generalizations too hard and fast; and consequently it was somewhat of a shock to the orthodox free trader* when John Stuart Mill made his famous statement that, in the case of a young nation protective duties were defensible,† on principles of political economy, when they were imposed "in hopes of naturalizing a foreign industry in itself perfectly suitable to the circumstances of the country." He went on to say that the differential advantage which one nation has over another in point of production is often owing to the fact that "it had begun it sooner."‡ But in making this statement Mill also said that such duties should be temporary. The whole question of the applicability, in a particular nation, of free trade or protection, must be studied out in accordance with the facts of the case.

The framers of the National Policy did not advocate it on the ground of economic theory. They acted entirely from the standpoint of practical expediency. They were desirous of building up the home industries, and the popular sentiment of the time was willing to make any sacrifice to accomplish this end. There was also a feeling that the adoption of a National Policy would make Canada independent of the trade depressions that affected other countries. But a protective policy, by unduly facilitating concentration, and at times congestion, of industry, may accentuate rather than minimize trade distrubances. The idea that protection entailed an immediate enhanced cost upon the consumer—which, however, might, in time, be repaid to him in cheaper goods—did not have much stress laid upon it. It was the producer, not the consumer, who was thought of. There was, however, some recognition of the fact that a permanent condition of protection was not desirable; for Sir Charles Tupper considered that fifteen years would be amply sufficient to place the Canadian manufacturers in a position of independence so that they could compete with foreign manufacturers.‖ The fifteen years have come and gone, and the "infant industries" are not yet willing to stand alone. This illustrates the fact that when once protection is adopted, in a country where a representative system prevails, it is exceedingly hard to remove it.

Some advocates of protection argue that an increased import duty is a matter of minor importance; because if foreign goods are imported it will be the foreign merchants upon whom, according to their hypothesis, the tax will fall. The advocates of Free Trade are, on the other hand, prone to claim that in all cases the consumer pays the tax.** The disputed question is as to the effect of the tax upon price. If it raises the price in the importing country, the result will

---

*The discussion is necessarily a mere outline. All that is desired, is to throw some light, from the theoretic standpoint, upon earlier Canadian protection.

†*E.g.*, Thorold Rogers, Political Economy, p. 235.

‡Mill's Principles, Vol. II., p. 538.

§Although Adam Smith had stated this.

‖"It was laid down by Sir Charles Tupper that fifteen years should be sufficient length of time to give the manufacturers an opportunity of getting improved plants, skilled workmen, and established chan els of trade." Speech of D'Alton McCarthy, M.P., at Barrie, January 11th, 1895.

**E. g. McCulloch's "Principles of Political Economy." Part II., ch. V.

4 T.H.

be that not only will the greater part of the tax be borne by the consumer, but there will also be paid by him, by way of increased price, a similar tax on the portions of the home-produced commodity of like nature which he consumes. But, on the other hand, the effect of the tax may be that the foreign producer will have to lower his price in order to obtain an entrance into the protected market;* here a portion of the tax will be paid by the foreign merchant. The subject is one of infinite complexity;† each case must be examined on its merits and in the process of such examination international price lists demand close scrutiny.

The iron and steel industry serves to illustrate the fact that the growth of an "infant industry" is not very rapid. Since 1887 the average rate paid on iron and steel imports has been 28.88 per cent. Notwithstanding this the imports of iron and steel were, in 1893, $13,199,525—a decrease in imports of $395,523, as contrasted with 1887.‡ Such being the condition of the imports, what is the condition of the home manufacture ? We find that in 1893 the total production of iron and steel in Canada amounted to $1,088,301, the total exports of iron and steel were $342,568, leaving for home consumption $745,933.§ It will, at this rate, take a long time to secure the Canadian market to the Canadian iron master;‖ it will take a much longer time to bring about the condition in which the consumer will be repaid by cheapened production for any sacrifices he may have made.

Aside from the advantages conferred by "a start," it is undoubtedly true that certain localities, and certain nations, are peculiarly suited for certain industries. But this consideration is apt to be overlooked, and the advantage the older nation has attributed solely to its "start."**

When protection is imposed it means that a paternalistic supervision of industry has to be attempted ; the Government, in determining which industries are suited to the country, which industries should receive protection, is much affected by the demands of the manufacturers ; and consequently industries are, from time to time, aided—the success and advantages of which are, at best, problematical.

One more question demands a passing consideration, and that is the Balance of Trade theory. Sir Leonard Tilley was an ardent believer in this theory ; to him it was the scientific buckler which served to cover all the crudities of the National Policy. The Balance of Trade theory comes down to us from the days of the Mercantilists. Many protectionists have discarded the theory, but in Canada it has, at times, exerted considerable influence. To the popular mind the theory seems conclusive ; by reasoning from the analogy of the individual income and

---

*c. g. The McKinley Tariff lowered the price of Canadian hay.

†An able treatment of this subject will be found in Prof. Edgeworth's article on "The Theory of International Values," in the *Economic Journal* for March, 1894, pp. 43-7.

‡See table IV., in appendix.

§The Statistical Year book 1893, chap. X. The Year Book does not give detailed data as to the total value of the iron and steel manufactures of Canada ; hence the figures used in this connection, are, at best, approximate.

‖The Dominion Statistician states that, "the decreases in imports are all in the groups the several articles composing which require the higher skill in manufacturing. The increases in imports are all in those groups which require the lower skill." Statistical Year Book, 1893, par. 638. However, the development in the industry has been so exceedingly *gradual*, that considerable time will elapse before the industry can stand alone. Notwithstanding the fact that pig iron is protected by a duty and a bounty, which in the aggregate amount to almost 100 per cent.—pig iron can be obtained in Alabama for $6.75 per ton—Canadian manufacturers are obtaining their pig iron from the Southern States. (*Vide* speech of Hon. Jno. Haggart at Orillia, February 4th, 1895.)

**Cf. List, p. 26.

expenditure it is assumed that when imports exceed exports that the country must be in a disadvantageous position and *vice versa*.* It is assumed that when the exports exceed the imports that the difference measures the net gain to the country, and that this constitutes a favorable balance of trade. The impossibility of perpetually maintaining a favorable balance of trade was demonstrated by Hume. The excess of exports does not of necessity constitute a favorable sign, for it may happen that, in a country where the exports exceed the imports, as in the case of India, this excess includes a large amount sent abroad in settlement of debts. Again, the balance of trade theory neglects the "invisible export" of transportation charges—an export which is very important to a carrying nation, such as England.† The seeming excess is largely due to the fact that the imports are usually valued at the place of their arrival, and hence the value includes transportation charge, while the exports being rated at the port of export are rated only at their market value there. But the greatest objection to this theory is that it assumes that debits and credits are settled directly between debtor and creditor. In practice it is found that the debtor nation has trade dealings ˏwith other nations ; and the debits and credits are settled in the majority of cases, not by direct payments of gold, but by bills upon the countries which are indebted to the debtor nation.‡

In 1885 Sir Leonard Tilley contended that the National Policy had tended to lessen the difference between the imports and the exports. We have already indicated the importance, from the revenue standpoint, of the import duties ; it might seem, then, a somewhat strange course of procedure, on the part of the financiers of the earlier period of the National Policy to desire to diminish the imports and increase the exports, for by so doing they would at the same time tend to decrease the revenue obtained from customs. It would seem as if, for the time, protection was more highly valued than revenue. Notwithstanding the efforts made to redress the "unfavorable balance of trade" the logic of facts shows how futile were the attempts of the believers in this theory, for, even when the National Policy was being congratulated for its success in this particular, we find that only during one year, 1880, did the exports exceed the imports, and then only by a million and a half, while during the period 1879-93 the imports have exceeded the exports by $294,669,078.§

---

*The theory is partially true. When the excess of imports necessitates an export of gold in order to cancel the indebtedness then this effect is of importance, for it exercises an effect upon prices. The other considerations advanced in the text must, however, be borne in mind.

†The imports of Europe exceed its exports by $1,200,000,000 annually ; and, paradoxical as it may seem, the imports of the world exceed its exports by $800,000,000 annually. The explanation of this fact is given throughout the paragraph. The transference of indebtedness in respect, *e. g.*, of the raising and repayment of loans, is an important element in the settlement of international balance.

‡See preface to "Everybody's Question," pp. 5-7. This is a pamphlet by Mr. G. H. Chambers, Chairman of the London and St. Katharine Docks Company (London, 1873, Effingham Wilson pubr.).

§See Table I. in appendix.

THE INFLUENCE EXERTED UPON THE CANADIAN TARIFF OF THE UNITED STATES

It is difficult to arrive at a conclusion on this question ceptable to all, for the question is usually discussed as a practic An answer to the question may be found in the Tariff H

To go back to the days preceding Confederation, we fin action of the American Congress in adopting a 50 per cent. r: the insertion of a 50 per cent. rate on spirits in the Canadian

Later we find that the action of the Canadian Government, the duties on tea and coffee was, so far as appears, caused : cedent action of the United States.† The events of this year f example of this influence. It was discovered later on in t United States intended to discriminate adversely against imported through Canada," and so provision was made‡ for commodities, when imported from the United States, the s imposed upon them when imported into the United States fr also draws attention to the question of retaliatory dutie: closely connected with the reciprocity phase of a protec retaliatory duties have been imposed by Canada, as in thi: provision is made for their imposition‖ dependent upon ι in general, been the action of the United States which ha: In these retaliatory duties there is an especial recognition of American Tariff.

Although the National Policy had a popular origin yc contended that the popular mind was influenced by the seei had attended the American " war Tariff; " then, as now, t tionists were ready to refer to the " beneficial influence tariff." Throughout the discussions which heralded in the N stress was laid upon the obtaining of "a reciprocity of Tariff to the south ;"** and one leading argument advanced in fav Policy was that it would obtain this " reciprocity of Tariffs." the American Tariff is again seen in the amending of the These changes are admittedly modelled upon the scale of iro: the United States.‡‡

But perhaps the most conclusive recognition of the infl can Tariff legislation is seen in 1894. It was somewhat late the Canadian Tariff Act was brought down ; and this was w be owing to a desire to await developments in the American to this there is seen, in the Canadian Tariff itself, much e that the American Tariff had been closely studied. Some approximation in point of Tariff rate on particular items ι comparative table given in a former portion of this essay.§§ may be cited. When the Finance Minister was speaking wi rate on live animals, he said : " Live animals . . . have

*See *The Toronto Leader*, the Government organ, for March 7th, 1859.
†*Vide ante*, p. 15. ‡35 Vict., Cap. 12. §*Vide*
‖*E. g.*, the provision for an export duty on lumber in the Tariff Act of 1894.
**See *Hansard* Debates of March 7th, 1878. ††*Vide ante*, p. 20.
§§*Vide ante*, in comparative table of Canadian and American duties, p. 45.

53

per cent., which is the percentage placed upòn live animals by the Wilson Bill and the Bill as emanating from the Senate Committee so far as it has gone."*

The facts that Canada and the United States have common trade interests—that the United States stands first on Canada's trade lists ;† that the territories are adjacent and that one is in a high stage of industrial development while the other is less highly developed industrially, would lead one to conclude that the Tariff Policy of the United States must exert an important influence upon the Tariff of Canada.

*Hansard, March 27th, 1894.

†In 1893 the total trade between Canada and the United States amounted to $108,988,856. England stood second with a trade of $107,385,718. (Statistical Year Book, 1893, p. 393.)